UP FROM THE FIELDS

JOHN H. BAILEY II

abbott press

Up from the Fields

ISBN: 978-1-4582-0404-2 (sc)
ISBN: 978-1-4582-0405-9 (e)
ISBN: 978-1-4582-0406-6 (hc)

Library of Congress Control Number: 2012909590

Abbott Press books may be ordered through booksellers or by contacting:

Abbott Press
1663 Liberty Drive
Bloomington, IN 47403
www.abbottpress.com
Phone: 1-866-697-5310

First Edition

Print information available on the last page.

Abbott Press rev. date: 03/08/2017

This book is dedicated to my mother, Lucille Bailey, whom I was not privileged to know, my father John L. Bailey, my God Mother, Edna Wattley Hoxie, and to the members of Flight F077 from Fort Campbell, Kentucky to South Vietnam on 16 December 1967.

CONTENTS

Preface..ix

Acknowledgements...xi

Chapter 1: The Mississippi Delta 1

Chapter 2: Texas By Sunlight.................................10

Chapter 3: A Year Of Change................................18

Chapter 4: From Boys To Men 27

Chapter 5: TET Offensive And The War Thereafter 48

Chapter 6: Challenge In Action 63

Chapter 7: Fixed Wing Aviator...............................96

Chapter 8: Brotherhood of Men............................107

Chapter 9: Mississippi My Way.............................115

Chapter 10: "I Touch The Future; I Teach" 131

Chapter 11: The Military Forces of Texas 147

Chapter 12: People Who Made A Difference 156

Challenge 164

More About the Author 167

Organizations... 170

PREFACE

As a small boy in 1949, having experienced enough pleasure and pain to last a lifetime, it became clear to me that the remainder of my formative years should be spent laying a foundation that would enhance my chances of living a life dominated by pleasures, where pain would be the exception and not the rule as I had witnessed in the lives of so many around me. I also realized after listening to and observing successful adults around me, that they all seemed to have a few things in common, first of all they believed in God and were dreamers, planners, organizers, and doers. And that's who I became at an early age. My faith engulfed me and my relationship with God was unflappable.

My dream was to become an aviator so I wrote a poem about it and kept it with me at all times. My plan was to complete high school, attend college, and attend flight school. At each level, being organized and having the self-discipline to do whatever it took to succeed became permanent in my mindset. To top it all off, my number one fan my father, who was only able to attain a third grade education, convinced me that you only fail when you stop trying. Therefore trying over and over again has never been a problem for me. I've tried putting my thoughts on paper a dozen times. Hope you'll find them worthy of reading.

ACKNOWLEDGEMENTS

It took many seemingly long arduous hours to complete Up From the Fields. I would first like to thank Amanda Roberts for the time she spent typing and putting the manuscript in the order requested by the publisher and Carmen Reed who gave invaluable assistance in editing the manuscript. I would also like to personally thank Mr. Alex Haley, author of Roots, whom I met by chance at the Side Track in Natchez, MS in the 80's, for encouraging me to go on and write this book, president J. Louis Stokes of Utica Junior College who after reading my article "Twelve Days Remembered" suggested that I expand it to a book, Mrs. Hatfield who taught History at Clear Creek High School who invited me to speak about the Vietnam War to her class each year until I retired in 2007, and last but not least, I want to thank Ruth, who gave me encouragement and listened to me talk about this project for many, many, many years.

CHAPTER ONE

The Mississippi Delta

IT WAS A MONDAY MORNING, the quiet seemed unusual, the fields were wet with morning dew for as far as the eyes could see and in the Mississippi Delta, with its flat terrain that seemed to be forever. From one direction we heard a not too familiar sound, from the other the sound of my father's straw boss's truck. He stopped, got out of the truck, and the two men started talking. At a distance I discovered that the other sound was an airplane, as usual I got terribly excited because you just didn't see many airplanes in the vicinity of Drew Mississippi.

Drew was like no other place on earth. To us it was our own little epicenter with earthquakes taking place each Friday through Saturday, when the masses of Sunflower County emerged on the little delta town giving it a carnival like atmosphere. Drew Mississippi was known for it's nearby prison named Parchman. In later years it became known as the former home of the Staple Singers, Archie Manning, my friends Robert Atkinson who flew F4's in Vietnam and earned three Distinguished Flying Crosses and Cleve McDowell who attended the University of Mississippi School of Law at a time when the University of Mississippi was not African American friendly. Over the years I have met many people from Drew doing things that my father could only dream of.

For us kids, many of whom seemed to have permanent

1

question marks on our faces, the Mississippi Delta seemed to have two faces of its own. One was warm, carefree and fun filled. The other was uncertain, cold, and with the charm of a cobra.

My family migrated to Mississippi from Maryland by way of Georgia and Alabama. Like many African American's they followed the fieldwork because it was what they had been taught to do. In the Delta, most black people were share croppers and lived on plantations where cotton was king, and cotton houses built to hold at least one bale of cotton looked like soldiers standing at attention from one end of the plantation to the other.

The unwritten contract between the plantation owner and the share cropper usually meant your family chopped the cotton, picked the cotton, and loaded the cotton on the truck or trailer so it could be hauled off to one of Eli Whitney's great inventions. The families received advances between March and November and received a settlement when all the cotton was picked and sold by the plantation owner. On the other hand there were day hands that usually lived in the city limits and were paid once per week to do farm work.

I didn't come from a large family. My grandfather, Rev. John H. Bailey, my grandmother, Mrs. Betty Johnson Bailey, my father, John L. Bailey, his sister, Mabelle Bailey Freeman, my mother, Lucille Clark Bailey, who died when I was two years old, and a half sister named Carrie M. Love. My only cousins that I knew of were my aunt's daughter, Betty, and her four children, Willie, Gloria, Brenda, Donald and the Staples family who were second or third cousins of my father. I got a chance to meet Oakie, Billie, and Flora Staples before we moved to Texas.

The T.A. Looney family owned the plantation on which I

was born. It was located approximately two miles from Drew. About one hundred yards from the front yard of our house was a railroad track that paralleled highway 49. About 100 yards behind our house was a bayou that provides many fond memories to this day.

T.A. Looney was a proud man who took good care of his people. He often rode a beautiful horse and would allow us kids to rub its head. My father was his lead day hand, meaning he kept the trucks and tractors in operating condition except for major maintenance, and was one of the equipment operators. Our house had four rooms and stood about three feet off the ground, behind the house was a big barn with a high ceiling and a tin roof. It was in that barn that I made my first parachute jump; only my parachute was a big umbrella used on a tractor. The minute the weight of my body pressed down on the handle, the thin braces gave way and the ride to the barn floor was expedited. I only made one jump.

The Looney house seemed quite big and had a loft. From time to time I would get to go up there and look at all the things and clothes that the almost grown Looney kids had out grown. We referred to the daughter as Bea Baby and the son as Baby Brother. Mrs. Looney was called "Ole Miss." As I grew older I thought maybe it was because she had attended the University of Mississippi, but never found out for sure.

Life on the plantation was what we knew, and as a five year old my job was to stay inside while my father and my grandmother were at work. My grandmother cooked and cleaned house for the Looneys. My father's best friend, Mr. Arthur Phipps, was their yardman and gardener. He and Mr. Buster Crockett were the only two of my father's friends whom I never saw take a drink of whisky or a drink of my dad's home brew. Mr. Phipps had a daughter a little older than I by the name of Lee Anna Phipps. Between she and Bea Baby I started reading quite early. Mr. Crockett had several children. I remember Charles and Joann best of all. After my father decided to put the big pasture that surrounded our quarters to use as a baseball field and organized a team we found that Mr. Crockett was one of the best pitchers in Mississippi. They played each Sunday after church. In some games Mr. Crockett pitched shutouts. He had a curve ball that dropped at the plate.

Of the festive moments during my young life were the holidays when the men got together and barbequed goats and ribs during the day and at night, in the absence of fire works, they rolled rags tightly and soaked them with kerosene, lit them and hurled them skyward. This they did to entertain the children of the families. I also received great Christmas gifts, one Christmas I received a pedaling car, another Christmas I received a pedaling airplane. I got my first whipping from my dad for riding the plane off that high porch and breaking off the propeller. My father cried with me. When I asked my grandmother why was he crying since it was I who had received the whipping, she said he sacrificed so much to buy me great toys and make me happy since I had lost my mother at such an early age. My reply did not help matters very much either, because I said I would rather have my mama than any toy. As I look back over those days I wonder how in the world could my dad afford to buy me expensive toys like that in the 1940's?

It wasn't long before we moved in with my grandmother because my dad had finally decided I needed another mother since he was gone almost every night. My grandmother lived on the other side of the railroad tracks. Across the secondary road from her house was a German POW Camp. The

Germans seemed strange to me. They would throw my toy guns away and say "No good, no good." They seemed to like my father because each Saturday he would go into town and buy them cases of canned pet milk. They loved milk. The only one I remember was one nicknamed Tom who would come by after work and talk to us before being escorted back inside. He looked at my grandmother in a strange way because she didn't look like the rest of us. She was lighter complexioned with green-gray eyes and a different grade of hair. Her eyes would change from green to gray when she was upset. That was quite often.

In October, of the year I turned six, my father and his new wife moved into a house across the street from Drew Colored Consolidated School. Her name was Ms. Willie Mae Williams. She was quite nice and very well organized. She worked for the Atkinson family. It was because of her that I met Robert Atkinson, who would end up being a life long friend. We had great times playing together while my new mom worked for his. His father had his own farm but lived in the city limits. His grandfather owned a drugstore and lived in one of the biggest houses in Drew. We referred to it as the "big house".

A day in the Atkinson household was much different from ours. Robert's mother, Mrs. Miriam Atkinson, had strict rules. She made us take naps at the same time each day and would give us graham crackers and milk after our naps. I love graham crackers and milk to this day. So do my own children. Another difference was what we did many Saturday afternoons. That was movie time and she would take us to the only movie house in town fondly referred to as the "picture show". Because of the temper of the times Robert would go downstairs and I upstairs to watch the same movie and we would meet at the ticket booth after the movie was over.

A funny, but great thing, happened one day after the movies. One of the teen age girls working the booth called us and gave us a huge box of left over popcorn and said there is something special for you two in the bottom. We couldn't wait to dump the popcorn and retrieve our surprise gift. The bottom of the box was covered with shinny new dimes. It seemed that they were the shiniest dimes I had ever seen.

I said lets count and divide them, Robert said you take them and use them for lunch money when you go to school and I did that and I ended up with a shoe box full of dimes as time flew by and a lot of love in my heart for all people. Black, White, you name it.

It wasn't long before I lost Willie Mae as a mother and was again alone with dad. Grandmother, who had left the Looneys, moved into town following daddy, her only son, now she worked for the Otha Sheridan family. Grandma lived in a one-room house on their property and I went to live with her. That was when I met Sammy and Theathel Wells. Their father was Mr. Sammy Wells Sr. and their Mother was Mrs. Ethel Wells. They were great people who treated me like their own child. Whenever my grandmother went away to St. Louis, MO to stay with her only granddaughter when she was having her babies the Wells family would take care of me. Once she left and never came back. That's when my father, who had found his second wife after my mother, came and took me back to the Looney place, where we stayed until we moved away to Texas, my dream state because I always liked western movies.

As I became older things seemed much different. Mama wouldn't allow me to wear shorts and I very seldom got to see my friends in Drew. A day I'll never forget was when I decided to go down the hill to the bayou and throw rocks into the water. I saw three colored teenage girls on the other side looking at me. The taller one said "Hey little boy. What's your name?" I said "John." "John what?" she asked. "John Bailey." I replied. She started walking towards the water asking, "What is your daddy's name?" I said "John L. Bailey." The teenager, who was now waving both hands in the air and jumping up and down, said, "Your mama's name is Lucille and she died about six years ago." I said, "Yes. How do you know that?" She said, "She was my mama too. I'm your sister Carrie." I then panicked and started running toward her. They calmed me down and told me to meet them at the footbridge about a quarter mile away. There we met and cried and I took the girls home with me to meet my new mama, Sarah Tibbs Bailey.

After they left my mama looked at me and said I was too black to have a sister that light skinned. When daddy came home he set the record straight. Carrie was my mother's daughter and I was her brother. She spent many weekends with us while we were still living in Mississippi. Carrie loved basketball and when my daddy and his friends would get in the bayou to san for fish, she and her friends were right in there with them. Those were fun times. They not only caught fish, they caught turtles, snakes, eels, and an occasional bullfrog. They kept the fish, killed the snakes, and threw everything else back into the water. If certain people were among the sanners, turtles were also kept since they made great soup.

One Saturday morning a shinny car with Texas license plates pulled up to our house. My step mom, Sarah, was as happy as I was when I saw my sister, Carrie, for this was her baby brother, Jack Johnson Tibbs (Rev. J.J. Tibbs), whom she had not seen since he left Mississippi going into the Army.

With him was his wife, Izora, a tall good-looking Texan who had spent her teenage years between Mexia and McKinney, Texas. He was now a preacher and she was a musician and great singer.

It wasn't unusual for them to show up two or three times a year. Because I was older now she insisted that I leave Mississippi and come with them to Texas where things were better for colored people. When she told me I could go to football games and not have to stand on the outside of the stadium and watch the game I was ready to go. For you see, my grandmother and I spent many Friday nights standing outside the Drew stadium so I could watch the football games. My grandmother was great. She would pop popcorn and peanuts and take sodas to the game so I could be like everyone else. I don't know if Drew Colored Consolidated School ever got funded for a football team, but they had great basketball teams. The principal, Professor Hunter, insisted on having a team and even having the school acquire a building that was intended for a second movie house as a gym so the team would not have to play outside during the winter months.

My father would not tell me what was up, but he insisted on taking me to see all of our friends over the course of a three-week span. And then he decided it was time to eat my pet pig, Tom, and my pet chicken, Firestone. I started thinking, Tom and Firestone are gone, what's going to happen to my dog Brown Eye. The name was not only because his eyes were brown, but because he was white all over with a brown patch covering his left eye, the tip of his tail and his ears with one brown spot on his back. After my mom died, dad would leave me at home with him when he went to work. Dad said Brown Eye wouldn't let me get too close to the fireplace or go out of the house and he was right. Whenever I went near the door he would get between me and the door and start starring at me.

Daddy finally told me why we were visiting everyone, we would be catching the bus for Texas in a couple days, but I couldn't tell anyone. We had three more places to visit. My mama's grave, his friend "Big Junior" who owned night clubs in Drew, and his friend John Taylor, who's son was our barber. All went well but one. It seemed that the cemetery where my mother was buried six and a half years earlier was now a cornfield because the church had burned down. So we just threw the roses we had picked all over the field. When asked what we were doing by the property owner I spoke up and told him and he said, "I don't know what you are talking about."

After we drove off my father said "I'm glad I'm getting you out of Mississippi. You don't speak to white men in that tone." I simply said that he would be upset too if he couldn't find his mother's grave. I have spent a lifetime wondering if we were looking for the church and cemetery at the wrong place.

My dad parked the truck in the Looney shed, gave his shotgun to another of my stepmother's brothers who lived on the Looney place and the next morning we caught the bus heading south on highway 49. When the bus stopped I was holding Brown Eye. The bus driver stepped to the door to take our money and said "Boy you can't put that dog on this bus." Before I could say anything daddy nudged me and gave me that you had better not say a word look. I rushed to the back of the bus where we had to sit according to customs and watched Brown Eye run behind the bus until I could no longer see him. I then slumped down in my seat and cried myself to sleep.

Chapter Two

Texas By Sunlight

After crossing the Mississippi River at Greenville Mississippi it seemed to take forever to cross the state line from Arkansas into Texas. I remember my dad shaking me and saying, "Wake up! We are in Texas." The first loud, squeaky words out of my mouth were "I don't see any cowboys." Everybody on the bus thought that was funny, except me. I was dead serious. As we exited the bus at our destination, McKinney, Texas, one of the passengers with a big grin on his face said "Hey Junior, forget the cowboys. You'll find the cowgirls are much more fun." He was right, but I didn't know what he meant at the time.

To be eight years old and have to go through such a noticeable transition in life took some getting used to. In a matter of hours I went from being extremely careful of what I said, what I did, and how I interacted with people to having kids my own age who were Hispanic and white living on the same street as I did and treating me like just as Robert Atkinson and I treated each other. My first week in McKinney a carnival came to town. It was my first. I had never had so much fun. I wished all of my friends in Mississippi could have been there. People of all races were there enjoying the rides, the games, the food and no one seemed to care about how black I was. Black kids in McKinney had new bicycles, black families had televisions and it seemed that every household had at least one automobile and most were property owners. My God mother's land at 913 Rockwall Street extended a whole block, from Rockwall Street to Lindsey Street. On the fence rows we raised grapes, along the sides there were peach trees, plum trees, apricot trees, and in the back yard there was an apple tree which I slept under many nights on my little green Army cot dad had bought for me from the Army Surplus Store. My dad, Uncle Jack Tibbs and I built a storage house in the back yard that would become the mount for my basketball goal and a source of much needed shade for my friend George Howell Jr. and me during the hot summer days. Just as our fathers worked and hung out together, George and I played and hung out together. He was my best friend although I couldn't count the friends I gained on my fingers and toes. As an only child growing up in our household I needed that. My father often said he wished his lifelong friends, whom he left in Mississippi, could experience the esthetic overtones of McKinney's culture and her wealth of good and decent people of all walks of life.

Another thing about Collin County and McKinney, Texas was there seemed to be a sense of togetherness. The white high school football team and the black high school football team played on the same football field and no one stood outside the stadium watching the games unless they couldn't afford a ticket. The colored school even had a tennis court. And if you could carry a golf bag you could be a caddy at the local country club and earn good money for a kid. We were also able to work on the Flying M Ranch and ranches that farmed hay and onions in addition to cattle. There was always work for us. As I got older I took jobs with construction companies until I landed a job at Safeway which resulted from the only racially motivated incident I recall being involved in while growing up in McKinney.

My God Mother, Mrs. Edna Hoxie, my friend Willie D. Clayton, and I went shopping at Safeway. It was then the top of the line grocery store in McKinney. The manager was a Mr. Stevens. As we finished shopping and started to depart the store I saw a sign that said sign here to win a prize. Mrs. Hoxie had exited the building and my friend Willie D was behind her. I handed him the bag I was carrying and went back to the register for the prize. This young adult male came up to me and said, "What are you stealing boy?" Although I was a boy, I didn't like his tone of voice and replied by asking him "Who are you calling a boy?" He said "I saw you hand something out of that door to your friend and you're going to jail." Everything in that bag was paid for. I said, "We don't steal. We pay for what we want."

He demanded that I stand still while he ran out and told my God Mother and Willie D to bring the bags back inside. By now Mr. Stevens, the store manager had reached the front of the store and everything came to a head. He asked for a receipt and told us to go back to the cash register that we had checked out through. When we got there the clerk, who was also white, said "That's Mrs. Hoxie and her son, John. They paid for everything they have and they are regular customers. I know them well. I am also their insurance agent."

Mr. Stevens told the young man to apologize to us and he did, but Mrs. Hoxie said, "That's not enough. We are a good Christian family and you have these people looking at us like we are thieves. I think I'll sue Safeway." Mr. Stevens invited us to his office, by that time Mr. Lester, the only black employee at the store who was also our next door neighbor came in and told Mr. Stevens who my God Mother was. "She is the sister to Tom and Sam Wattley, the black family with the oil wells down in Mexia, Texas. She probably does have enough money to sue Safeway." Now that was all news to me. I finally found out why she never went to work. At that moment Mr. Stevens said "Why don't I just correct this by giving John a job." She agreed, I took the job and stayed there until I graduated from high school and joined the US Army. First I was a bag boy and then I was promoted to produce, which I enjoyed very much. Safeway became my first stop when home on leave from the Army.

McKinney was also a good place for my parents. Dad was hired by Ford Motor Company servicing customer's cars and trucks and my mom was hired by a restaurant called the Red Rock Inn. They worked at those jobs for the duration of their stay in McKinney, which lasted for about three years. Daddy started having foot and knee problems after a couple of years, which he said, were caused by all the cement floors at his job. His friend Mr. George Howell did the best he could to keep daddy from returning to Mississippi, but after a few years in Texas, that's exactly what he did.

When I started school I probably noticed the greatest of all the changes I would experience. Black children were speaking Spanish because it was requires and I had never read or talked so much about Shakespeare until I attended Doty. And then there was football, the favorite Friday night past time from September to the end of November. Since E.S. Doty High School was so small if you were big enough you could try out for the team even if you were in Junior High. In addition to football, Doty High had track and field, basketball, and a choir and band. I lettered in everything except band. I couldn't figure out a way to play football and be in the band at the same time.

We had great, very proud and highly motivated teachers at Doty. Our principal during my early years was Professor John W. Fenett. His wife, Mrs. Fenett, was also an educator and very active in the community and the church.

At Doty High, like most schools, some of our teachers were super stars and made everlasting marks on our lives. First on my list was Coach Leonard Evans, our head football coach, basketball coach, and track coach. Coach Evans became a father figure to me after I lost my father in 1957. He gave us quite a scare when a blowtorch exploded in his hands and seriously burned most of his body. Members of our choir insisted on going to the hospital and standing near the window to his room and singing our school song "Good Ole Doty Blue." The song never sounded so good.

Next on my list was Mrs. Aquilla C. Johnson, our choir director, who also taught social studies. Continuing my list of favorites were Coach Mitch Jackson, Principal Rueben Johnson, Mr. A. A. Malvern, the band director and chemistry teacher, Mrs. M. Howell Brown, our English and Spanish teacher, Ms. Irene Clayborne, who wasn't much older than we were, Mrs. Julia Evans, Mrs. A. A. Malvern and Mrs. Ruth Doty.

Many of them now have schools named in their honor in the city of McKinney. So influential were these teachers, that we couldn't wait to get to school so we could be around them, and we didn't want to go home at the end of the day. We wanted to grow up and be successful like they were. Coach Evans liked to take us to Hamilton Park to play basketball so we could see and appreciate the new all black neighborhood that surrounded the school campus. As we would leave you could hear students pledging to live in neighborhoods like that when they grew up.

Doty High School, with its Gym behind it, was centered on a piece of land that had houses surrounding it on three sides. We called it the horseshoe. Many of the homes on the horseshoe were occupied by teachers. The who is who in McKinney's black neighborhood in the 1940's and 50's. The most famous home on the horseshoe was the home of Rev. ML Bailey and his family. Famous because Melvin, Benjamin, and Beatrice lived there and most of all famous because Mrs. Bailey decided to convert her garage into a small store that catered to school aged children. They sold candy, cookies, ice cream, sodas, and pickles. You get the picture. Best of all we were able to go there and shop during our lunch period and if you were in high school you could go there during recess.

Other than school, the next most important thing in our lives was religion. Although I had wanted to be Catholic since spending time in St. Louis and playing on the church campus every day, there were no black Catholic churches in McKinney. Most churches were Baptist. There was one Methodist church that was home to many of the teachers and other middle class blacks in McKinney and several Pentecostal churches. My folks were Baptist and we were in church three times on Sunday and Mission, prayer meeting and choir practice during the week. Everything evolved around the school and the church. To keep the young men occupied we had a Boy Scout Troop, Explorer Post, and a boys club. There was always something for us to do and during fair season we always went to the Texas State Fair, the greatest fair on Earth and that same weekend we went to the Cotton Bowl Stadium to watch Prairie View take on another historically black college. It was at the State Fair that James Wattley Jr. and I lucked out and ended up on the front cover of Ebony Magazine. We were leaning on the front of the stage when Lavern Baker was singing. We both bought several copies and even autographed a few.

It was in the Cotton Bowl stadium that I got a chance to see Clem Daniels, a graduate of Doty High play for Prairie View, for the first time. He would go on to become and exceptional player for the Oakland Raiders football team. It's wonderful knowing he is alive and well in Oakland, the last time I saw him at a Doty reunion he looked great.

At that point in my young life things couldn't have been any better. I knew who and where I was and who I wanted to become. We all made up our minds that when we grew up our homes would be no less than the ones we had seen in Hampton Park when going there to play basketball. My parents and teachers taught me what it would take to get there. Thanks to hard times in Mississippi I wasn't afraid of work and my people skills were exceptional for a kid.

For most of my time in McKinney I lived at 913 Rockwall Street with my God Mother, Mrs. Edna Hoxie. She was a little brown lady with a few freckles and the prettiest long black plats I had ever seen. Rumor had it that her family, the Wattleys, had some Native American blood in them. They had migrated to McKinney from Mexia, a small town not too far from Houston. Each summer I would go there with Mr. Deid Johnson to work land. It seemed to take forever to travel from McKinney to Mexia, especially pulling a trailer with an ornery ole mule named Sam on it. We never stayed more than a few days. Then we took the long trip back to McKinney. I traveled with eyes wide open since my God Mother told me if I went to sleep during the trip so would uncle Deid who just happened to be driving.

The most exciting thing about being a young boy in Texas was Friday Night Football. Texans loved their football then as much as they love their football now. I couldn't wait to get old enough to play for the Doty High School Bobcats.

McKinney's black community was broken down into three major neighborhoods: Northeast McKinney was home to the part of town known as Lewisville, West McKinney was called the Run, and Southeast McKinney east of the railroad tracks was known as Rockwell, with Rockwell Street being the main thru fare.

Favorite apparel for boys seemed to be Levi blue jeans, white t-shirts with pockets, and white Bucks. Our favorite cars were the 1955, 56, and 57 Chevrolets, candy apple red with chrome plated Rims and white side wall tires, although none of us owned one. Five of us thought we would become a singing group and Paul Brown and I hoped to some day become pilots. All of my friends had great parents who opened their hearts and arms to me. I'm grateful that some are still with us.

Chapter Three

A Year Of Change

As the summer of 1954 came to an end my step mom began to get restless in Texas because McKinney was so different from the life she had enjoyed in Mississippi. As a race there was no comparison to how we were treated in Texas, which was much better, on the other hand my parents' social life left much to be desired. Collin County was dry therefore there were no nightclubs, no juke joints, no all negro baseball leagues. Social life in McKinney, Collin County, Texas was built around the church and the school. As a kid I had no problems with either, but John L. and Sarah Bailey needed a place to let off steam and before I knew it a big truck with Mississippi license plates was parked in front of our house. This caused mixed emotions for me. I was devastated. But because my uncle Jack, known to the Texas religious community as Rev. Doctor J.J. Tibbs, had announced his intentions to move to California after the birth of their daughter Loretta, my step-mom figured she had nothing to keep her in Texas. My God Mother, Mrs. Hoxie, a long time resident of McKinney and my father got together and came up with a plan for me. I would travel with them to Mississippi, but would be back in Texas in time to start school in the fall of 1954. I rode on the back of the truck with the furniture and cried all the way to Texarkana, Arkansas where we stopped and dad bought me everything I asked for, cookies, candy, sodas, you name it. Dad expected to see joy on my face, but joy for me was in a place called McKinney.

Upon arriving in a little farming community called Beulah, Mississippi, I started working on the farm and looking for new friends. On the farm thirteen year olds worked like grown men. The plantation we moved to was actually about five miles from the little town of Beulah, the community was known as Mound City. I was told its name came from a large Indian Burial Mound that was covered with more stone arrowheads than I had ever seen in my thirteen years on this earth.

The place was different from the Looney place in the Mississippi Delta where farm hands lived in houses that were in no particular order. Here the houses were lined up along a long dirt road that led from the gravel road known as Route 1 to a huge wooded area simply known as the woods. The houses were evenly spaced. Behind each house was a pump used to get water from the earth, farther away from the back of the house was an outhouse, to the right of the house was that occupant's garden space, hog pen and chicken house so we could raise our own food. Directly across the road in front of your house was the cotton field you were responsible for working, with the cotton house at the opposite end of the long cotton rows aligned at equal distances on another dirt road that paralleled the road the houses were on. It was clearly a planned plantation community. At the end opposite the woods along the gravel road was a country store, church, a cemetery, and of course those huge Indian Burial Mounds covered with arrowheads. Everyone's mailbox was grouped along that gravel road. Ours was Route 1 Box 135. When school started that's where we would stand and wait for the bus. Many days I would be the only kid standing there, but we picked up other kids as the bus passed other plantations in route to Pace Colored School, In Pace, Mississippi.

Just about everyone in Pace was black it had no industry, just clothing stores, grocery stores, a barbershop, and nightclubs, one was owned by Auwilda Mason's mom. The best thing there was the school with its staff of exceptional teachers headed by Principal Willie Dean Smith.

Among my first friends in Bolivar County Mississippi was Jesse L. Reason, tall thin and quite ambitious. It was Jesses who made sure I met the kids who were the who is who in Pace and the surrounding area. After a short month or so I had no problems wanting to stay there until time for high school back in Texas and maybe even longer. Jesse Reason and I would walk from the rural area where he was living to Pace and back. One day we decided to take a short cut across a large rice farm as we walked along the bank of one of the long irrigation ditches we decided to take a swim. As we undressed down to our skivvies and walked to the water's edge preparing to jump in, a water moccasin headed straight towards us from the other side. We both said snake, quickly dressed, and walked in silence for at least half a mile before Jesse asked if I was a good swimmer. I asked him why and he said he was counting on me saving him if he got in trouble. I said that was funny because I was depending on you saving me. We came to an agreement that God had sent the snake, because he wanted to spare us for some greater good. Jesse is now a minister in Chivago.

In a matter of time Jesse had introduced me to his sister Lucille, I liked her very much because she shared my mother's name, and his cousins Leon Halbert and Sylvester Walters who lived near him. In Pace he introduced me to Edgar Jackson, his sister Nell, Auwilda Mason, the Vick brothers, Billy Lefore, and Charlie Scott. When school started I met the rest of his friends. Among them were Doris and Elise Townsend and of course Alma Rose and Baby Dean, daughters of the school principal, Professor Willie Dean Smith, who loved his school, his staff, and his students and was an all around great human being. We had talent shows, a great little basketball team and were one of the few schools in the area that had its own version of gymnastics. We had great times tumbling and flipping and no one ever received injuries.

Some of the things I'll always remember about that time in my life was the day this tall girl approached me and everyone stopped what they were doing and looked at us. It was a Saturday and as usual people gathered around the country store, they all stared at us in suspense. Finally she said "Hey little ole big eyed boy, do you know who I am?" After hearing her voice and getting a good look at her I said, "Yes. You're my sister." And it was on. We must have hugged for ten minutes. This time she said, "I'm not going to let you get away again, I'M staying." After talking to my dad and step mom they agreed to let her stay. After a couple of weeks Sarah finally said since Carrie was almost nineteen years old she was grown and our house wasn't big enough for two women. Carrie moved in with a family my dad had befriended since moving back to Mississippi. I would see her as often as I could, usually on weekends.

All of the boys in the area loved basketball, baseball, and football. You pretty much only had to have a ball of some sort to play basketball but the goal would often times be a five gallon can with the top and bottom cut out. Football on the other hand was quite a different story. We played with old shoes, cans, and many times the very small footballs you could buy for less than a dollar. The closest black school with a football team was the Colored High School in Cleveland, Mississippi.

I had finally accepted the fact that I might not be returning to Texas as promised. Life improved when Leon and Sylvester's parents purchased new automobiles and we were able to use them to make frequent trips to Cleveland for movie night. Leon and Sylvester were older and could drive. About once per week we visited the all black movie there that was always packed. The only problems we encountered were the usual harassment a group of black kids riding in a new car could expect. Once an older couple waved down a highway patrolman and accused us of trying to run them off the road. I think because we were all clean cut and showed proper respect to the Officers, they decided to let us go. This was the beginning of what would be an unpleasant year in the state of Mississippi.

The young man who lived closest to me was named Lee Ingram, Jr. He was about three years my senior. He often encouraged me to leave and return to Texas because he liked everything I had told him about Texas. Before I knew it, he was joining the Air Force so he could get away from Mississippi and see the Texas that I so vividly described to him. Shortly after completing Boot Camp and MOS Training, Lee was lost in a boating accident. I felt terrible about that for a long time, it was like he was gone because I bragged about Texas so much. I stopped talking about McKinney, Doty High School and it's football team and tennis court.

On Saturdays I resumed my old habit of going to the country store and hanging out. It was our Mall and our Skating Rink. One Saturday as I sat outside the store this young Caucasian man got out of his pickup truck and walked up to me and asked if I could read. I told him yes. He reached into his shirt pocket and handed me a folded, beat up piece of paper and said "I'm going to call everybody over here and I want you to read it to them so they will know I'm somebody special." I said "Yes sir." As he asked everyone to come over I scanned the paper. It was his honorable discharge from the US Army. As I started to read he stopped me and said "Stand up on the back of my truck so they can all see and hear you." He had been a truck driver in the Army and was discharged with the rank of Private First Class. He was proud of his service and we were all proud for him. He looked at me and said, "Here, take this six bits. I'll be back next Saturday and you can make some more of my hard earned money." It was like he wanted to be nice to me but just couldn't do more than say hello when he drove past me walking on Route 1, which I did many times going back and forth to visit Jesse Reason and the Robert Lee Jones family.

The now stranger to me did manage to do me a favor, he told my dad's boss that I was a good reader and was probably good at math and should be hired to weigh and keep the records for the day hands who came from within the city limits to work on the plantation. I was given that job, but was still required to help my stepmother work her assigned acreage.

1954 was not just a difficult year for farm work but also just for being a black teenager in the state of Mississippi. Some very mean spirited Caucasian males started stopping by the country store trying to pick up black women and girls. One Saturday afternoon my neighbors and I were at the store hanging around outside and going inside only to purchase sodas, cookies, and candy when I spotted a little key chain with a view graph on it. You held it up to the light and looked into it and whatever was in it came to view. In my view was a young woman in a bathing suit, and yes, she was white. Black girls were not put in the view graphs. As I looked into it a hand snatched it away. The next thing I knew the man was saying, "What are you doing looking at a white girl?" He then threw it down and stomped on it. I said "They don't put black girls in view graphs and they sold it to me in the store, you owe me the money I paid for it." As he pushed me I pushed his hand off of me and ran home to tell my daddy what had happened. This person wouldn't let it be. He followed me home in his truck and told dad what I had done and to send me out so he could whip me.

Dad said, "I'm his daddy and I'm the only man who is going to whip him. He's a good boy; he goes to school, and never gets into trouble. I'll just have him apologize to you." I stepped onto the porch and said "I'm sorry sir." but I really wasn't because I felt that he didn't have the right to destroy anything I had paid my money for, and he didn't have the right to touch me. The next time I read the discharge notice for Bo I told him what happened. He told me the view graph breaker was simply a mean person and that I should do my best to stay away from him.

Soon we were preparing to go back to school and I couldn't go anyplace after sundown. That was never a problem before. One of the greatest songs out that year was Pledging My Love by Johnny Ace; we all enjoyed that song so much. I even had the nerve to sing it at one of the Talent Shows. Some kid from Rosedale, Mississippi came in first place and I came in second. Soon Christmas rolled around and I got up early as usual. It was great because I received a basketball and goal and could discard the five-gallon bucket I had been using as a goal. Later that day we were all saddened by the news that singer Johnny Ace had killed himself in Houston, TX playing a game with a handgun called Russian Roulette. The song Pledging My Love soared even higher. On a January day in 1955 when we least expected it, Mr. Smith returned to campus with the best looking basketball uniforms we had ever seen. They were gold with blue numbers on the jerseys that really stood out and made us feel like we were in Madison Square Garden as we played in the little wooden gym with the low ceiling.

Meantime on the home front my step mom Sarah surprised me by saying that we were going to Texas to visit Uncle Jack and Aunt Izora before they moved to California. We stayed a couple of weeks before returning. While there I promised my friend George Howell Jr. and cousin James Wattley Jr. that I would be back soon. I didn't realize just how soon that would be.

We returned to Mound City in July 1955. On August 28 1955 Emmett Till was murdered and thrown in a river in Money, Mississippi. His mother made sure the word of what had happened to her baby was spread around. My father panicked. I was his only living son. He said I had to be kept safe to keep his father's name going. I was back in McKinney before I knew it, just in time for the 1955 football season, but would never see my father alive again.

Doty High School was an all black school filled with great athletes with very big hearts. My first year there we began practice with leather helmets, hand me downs from McKinney High School. Coaches Evans and Jackson saw something in us and believed we could play football. One day Coach Evans returned from District with new helmets and new jerseys. From that point on we thought he walked on water. Our first game started on the wrong foot. Denton beat us 45 to 0. The ride home was long and quiet but the next three seasons were great. We won district each year, went to bi-district one year and the state quarterfinals one year. Other than my first high school football game, which I will always remember, I will never forget the 112 to 0 spanking we put on a school near Greenville, Texas in 1958. That will teach them to tolerate a sign that says, "Welcome to Greenville, the Blackest land, the Whitest people." After the game we discussed the sign. One of the Greenville players asked me if it would make me happy if the sign said the Blackest land and the Blackest people. After thinking about it I wouldn't have liked that either. Little did I know the score 112 to 0 would come up again in my life, on a different playing field. Because of the big hearts of my Doty teammates I wish I could have had them all there with me when 112 to 0 would once again appear.

At each point in my life, there was the village it took to raise a child. That village consisted of close relatives, teachers, coaches, friends, church members, the band, members of our championship choir, and members of our Friday Night Football Clan who often spent time speaking of Clem Daniels the pride of Doty High Football who was ahead of us by a few years. Favorites during my playing years were: Alfred Perry, Thomas Jackson, Dennis Palmer, Joe Palmer, William Thornton, Charles Newman, C. B. Allen, Jesse McGowan, Oscar Turner, Linda Finney, Jimmie Johnson, Willie Cecil Johnson, Patricia Berry, Alice Faye Johnson, Barbara Ann Reed, Melvin L. Bailey, Cookie Johnson, Otis Holley, Nancy Wattley, Norman W. Ellis, Elmer Reed Jr., Madeline Berry, James Wattley Jr., and John Henderson.

Chapter Four

From Boys To Men

THE DOTY HIGH CLASS OF 1959 was the largest graduating class in the history of Doty. Few of us had the funds to pay for college but some of us were offered scholarships, thanks to Coach Evans and Melvin Brown. My scholarship was offered by Bishop College, which had recently moved to Dallas, Texas from Marshall. The plan was I would go there during the summer months, try out for choir, and if selected I would be given a scholarship as a male soloist. All went well until I sat at the piano and started echoing my baritone voice across the room. That was when the choir director decided to keep time by tapping me on the thigh. I could only scoot so far away from him on a piano stool. I called home and told my God Mother what he was doing and she told me to tell him I wasn't comfortable with that. I did, but he didn't seem to hear me. I stood up, told him what he could do with the scholarship, and caught the bus home, which was only about 18 miles. Within a few weeks I had joined the US Army along with Bobby Owens, Otis Holley, Louis Roberts, Mack Bollin, and Lonnie Roberts.

After testing, physicals, and briefings we were put on a train and sent to Fort Carson, Colorado. It was the first time I had ever seen mountains move, that was crazy. The mountains farthest away from us seemed to be keeping pace with the train. Of Course it was an illusion. At Fort Carson we saw something else we had never seen, snow and hail in July (Pikes Peak). As soon as we made our minds up that we liked the place we were told there wasn't enough room for us at Fort Carson and we would be sent back to Texas for Basic Training, Fort Hood, Texas to be exact. One July evening we boarded several old C-47 airplanes that were civilian owned and headed for Fort Hood. Can you imagine how lucky we were to fly on this WWII icon in 1959? I took a seat by a window so I could see out of the airplane.

During the engine run up I felt something fall into my lap that caused sure panic for me, and the soldier sitting to my left. It was the window. We both started screaming like kids on a farris wheel. A crewmember came with some glue and green tape and fixed the window. I was looking at him with such concern that he explained that the tape was simply there to hold the window until the glue dried. From Fort Carson to Fort Hood I only watched the window, not the scenery on the outside.

Upon reaching Fort Hood everything changed. We were being called names like "Meat Head", "Dummy", and a few others we had not become accustomed to. We were assigned to the First Armored Rifle Battalion, 50th Infantry. Our patch, which we wore over our pocket, said "Hell on Wheels" although we seldom rode anywhere. We soon changed it to "Hell on Heels" because our heels took a beating from all the walking and running around that sprawling Army base.

Our Company Commander was a Captain Beverly and our Platoon Sergeants were Sergeant Goodson and Sergeant Contreras. I would see Sergeant Goodson again after I had achieved the rank of Major. He seemed proud of my achievements. After about three weeks at Hood we were allowed to visit the small Enlisted men's clubs in our unit areas. They sold weak beer and cherry cokes. I drank plenty cherry cokes, but couldn't stand the taste of beer. A week later we were allowed to go to the base service club, Fiddlers on the Roof. There we saw live shows that included women, games to play, and desks to sit at and write letters home and of course television. I think the highlight of Basic Training was when every recruit there marched into the base football stadium to watch the Fort Hood Tankers play a local college game of football. You would think we were Texas A&M Cadets because we stood and chanted the whole game. Those were proud days for us. We were in the US Army and were being paid $72.00 per month and none of us had ever heard the name "Vietnam". It didn't help to learn that the great Elvis Pressley had taken his basic training just across the field from where we were. Each time I was caught looking in that direction I was dropped for push-ups for wreckless eyeballing sacred ground. Even that paid off for me because when we took our first PT test I scored the highest in the company.

After my stint in an Infantry Unit I received my first disappointment in the Army. I thought I would be attending photography school but ended up in clerk school at Aberdeen, which turned out to be ok for me. About half way through my training my friends and I were heading to the service club when I saw this beautiful young lady standing under a tree looking around. I said to them "She looks like my girlfriend from Texas." They laughed and said "Yeah right." About the same time my eyes met hers and we started running towards each other and hugged. "What are you doing here?" I said. She smiled and said, "All of my friends told me not to let you get away from me and I agreed." After I received the signed document from my God Mother saying I could get married, we did just about a week later on 11 November 1959, and she returned to Texas.

From Aberdeen I went to Fort Bragg, North Carolina to attend Jump School and an assignment to the 82nd Airborne Division. Jump school was a piece of cake but the instructors were even wilder than the ones at basic training. We were all referred to as legs because we had not earned our jump wings. My Instructor was Sergeant Collins, a man feared by all jump students because he stayed in our faces, threatening us. Once my wife and I were walking down Hay Street in Fayetteville and met him on the street. I tried to introduce him to my wife, but his reply was "I don't want to meet no damn leg wife. Get away from me. Get away from me #246."

246 was my assigned student number that I wore on the front of my helmet during training. I couldn't imagine that he could remember my number. That Monday morning he remembered it again and said "246 fall out and drop and knock out fifty pushups for trying to introduce me to your leg wife." If I only could have bumped into him after Officer Candidate School, Flight School, Jump Master School, two tours of duty in Viet Nam, and a degree from Embry-Riddle I'm sure he would have been as proud of me as I was of him.

At Fort Bragg I was assigned to the Division Supply Office as a Records Clerk. My Platoon Leader was a Lieutenant named Jack W. Cowlishaw. My Platoon Sergeant was a WWII Veteran Paratrooper with a Combat Infantryman's Badge and two Combat Jump Stars on his Master Parachutist Wings. His name was Arthur C. Radosch who hailed from Chicago. They were perfect examples of professionalism and people skills. There were four of us blacks in their platoon, Shaw, Montgomery, Freeman, and me. We became the best of friends. Shaw met and married the love of his life in Fayetteville. Montgomery and Freeman remained single. I have wanted to locate them over the years, but have been afraid to look for their names on the Vietnam Wall. Other than jumping out of perfectly good airplanes and participating in countless field exercises together, including the 100 miles Stonewall Jackson March from South Carolina to Fort Bragg after a joint exercise with the 101st Airborne Division our greatest day came when President Kennedy came to town.

The entire Division of approximately 16,000 strong formed at Pope Air Force Base near Bragg to be viewed by the President. Being young enlisted men with too much time on our hands we decided to take up a collection of $1.00 from any trooper who wanted to participate, and give it to the one trooper who had a chance to speak with the President and was bold enough to tell him he needed a haircut. Well, as fate would have it he stopped in front of me, put his right hand on my shoulder and said, "You are a good looking paratrooper. Hang in there." Those words spoke volumes to me. They literally changed my life. The next week I purchased three more pairs of jump fatigues and a pair of new Cochran jump boots. But I didn't get them with the money I won in that pot. When he touched me I froze. I couldn't say a word, my mouth wouldn't work. I earned the money for the fatigues and boots pulling KP or Kitchen Police for poor little rich guys who just happened to spend their time as draftees in the 82nd Airborne Division but didn't care to pull guard duty or KP.

The rest of my time at Fort Bragg was spent jumping out of airplanes, participating in Division Readiness Exercises, Field Training Exercises, and being on alert for Dominican Republic and other hot spots around the world. We shared Fort Bragg with the newly founded Special Forces "Green Berets", the 18th Airborne Corps HQ, and a handful of non Airborne Units, but the 82nd Airborne Division "All Americans" was the US Army's STRAC force at Fort Bragg, North Carolina, and we made sure everyone knew it.

A day in the life of a young enlisted paratrooper included spit shinning the area around his bunk, making sure everything in his wall locker and footlocker was spotless and perfectly aligned and spit shining his jump boots until they hurt the eyes of passers by.

We memorized the numbers of Field Manuals, Technical Manuals, Army Regulations, Bulletins and Circulars so we could locate any information we needed. This knowledge came in handy for guard duty, soldier of the month boards and unit pride.

Occasionally someone was killed in a parachuting accident. Our senior enlisted leadership used those events as training aids to prepare us for dealing with death in combat. When you considered the number of deaths in a division with approximately 16,000 jumpers they were few and far between and usually were caused by paratrooper error while in the air or high winds. 1,250 feet doesn't give you much time to correct mistakes. While assigned to the 82nd Airborne Division I received promotions to Private First Class and Specialist Fourth Class, took my first college courses and two classes on General Aeronautics through the education center.

It was at Fort Bragg that I first paid attention to the culture of the Army officer, and liked what I saw. They all seemed to be at a much higher ethical, intellectual and moral level of existence than we were and rightfully so. Most were highly educated. They walked erect, looked you in your eyes when they talked to you and their word was always their bond. On their shoulders they wore gold or silver and on their ring fingers they wore their credentials, West Point Ring, College Ring, or Officer Candidate School Ring. If they were married, the college ring was worn on the left finger with the wedding band symbolizing marriage to the spouse, and to their Institution, and to the United States Army. The wives of West Pointers also wore a small version of their husband's West Point ring. Though they were paid higher salaries than enlisted soldiers the difference in income was the least of what set us apart, I was impressed.

In addition to graduating from Jump School, earning two promotions and getting into college, a most wonderful thing happened to me as a man. On 7 August 1961, Velma gave birth to Harriett, the first Bailey girl born in my family since 1916 when my father's older sister was born and only the third Bailey alive, her mother and I being the other two. She was a very quiet little girl who loved her mother and her tricycle. She didn't look like her mother nor me, but she had my complexion and from the description my father gave me of my mother, I think that is where her looks came from. She was born with a head full of thick, curly, jet-black hair and being her father gave new meaning to my life.

With a baby girl in our lives we needed a car so I re-enlisted for six years and took the money and paid down on our first car. It was a 1960 Corvair Monza, now I find myself in a position to have to perform KP or Guard Duty for someone at least three times per month to make sure I could cover all the bases without causing financial stress.

After a short leave to Texas as part of my reward for re-enlisting, I was met with the sad news that Sergeant Radosch had suffered a heart attack and died while I was gone. I had not felt pain of that magnitude since losing my father. The 82nd Airborne Division wasn't the same to me plus the Civil Rights movement was heating up and we were all quite tense. When I received orders for the 8th Infantry Division in Germany I had mixed emotions.

I took the family to Texas, reported to Fort Dix, New Jersey and boarded a KC 135 aircraft headed for Deutschland leaving behind a pregnant wife and the cutest little girl on earth.

My tour in Germany provided much insight to many events I had read about and afforded me the opportunity to visit many historical battle sights in Germany and several adjourning countries. The food, wine and people were great. My recurring thought was how could the likes of Hitler rear his deceptive head and poison the minds of so many intelligent and hardworking people. Upon arrival into Frankfurt, Germany we left the plane and boarded trains for our various destinations in Germany. I was being assigned to Headquarters 8th Infantry Division, Bad Kreuznach, Germany and because the 8th had one Airborne Brigade I was assigned to an E-5 Jump slot which meant I could continue adding jumps to my jump log and get promoted to Specialist 5th Class. It wasn't long before I learned that regardless to what kind of Division you were in the order of business was to remain skilled, tough, and ready around the clock (STRAC).

Because I was not an E-5, my wife could not accompany me at Government expense. She remained at home with her parents until our son, John H. Bailey III, was born and until I saved enough money to purchase their plane tickets and rent and furnish an apartment on the German economy.

Barracks life in Germany was a little different from barracks life in the States. In Germany we had bed check and every soldier had a certain time to be back to base, and every soldier not accompanied by his spouse had to live in the barracks though the Senior Non-Commissioned Officers had private rooms on each floor. It seemed that most of the soldiers who would be reduced in rank would have that unfortunate thing happen to them for missing bed check. The real sad reality was that many Sergeants reported to Germany wearing three stripes and two rockers and returned to the States minus the rockers, meaning they were reduced from pay grade E-7 to pay grade E-5. Not a good way to manage ones career.

Finally the day came when my family would join me in Germany. It was November 1962. What a sight seeing them come down that ramp from the airplane at Frankfurt airport. My life would be better, because I was clearly the family man type and needed to be a husband and father. My boss in Germany was a Captain Gerald T. Buckley. He was assisted by a Warrant Officer 2 Frank Breault and an E-5 named Troy Glenn Baker. They were a great team to work for. Our best friends in Germany were: Sergeant Freddie L. Johnson and his wife, Joan from Selma, Alabama.

Although the 8th was a Mechanized Infantry Division, it had one Airborne Brigade that was stationed in Mainz, Germany. That meant that all other key units in the Division had a few Airborne slots. Getting used to the German culture took a little extra effort for a black American from the South. The blacks at Bad Kreuznach all knew each other. The Senior NCOs would take turns hosting get-togethers on weekends where we played cards, pokeno, and ate great soul food. It seemed that although we were so far from our homeland, we had a little America right there with us. We had American churches, an American High School that provided us with high school football and basketball, and the number of American cars seemed to increase each year. My three years in Germany meant I was in the wrong place during the Civil Rights Movement. I was defending my country while at the same time not being there to stand up and be counted when being counted meant so much for our cause. Another bright spot was seeing my brother-in-law Rufus Johnson, Jr. and a future brother-in-law Lamon Sims.

About half way through our tour in Germany Christopher was born. Watching him grow and speak German and wear lederhosen was quite a treat. I'll never forget coming home from work one day to find Harriett, John, and Chris on the play grounds with their little German friends, all speaking German.

We visited quite a few countries while there. The most exciting was France. I learned a great deal about military leadership there. It came with the territory.

My promotion to E-5 put me in a position to practice power, authority, and leadership, and qualified us for military housing. The Cold War meant that our Division had to remain ready for combat and spend much of our time on Field Training Exercises or placing our Initial Ready Force and Division Ready Force units on alert. The best day of that three-year tour was 10 October 1963 when Chris joined us. The absolute worse was 22 November 1963, the date of the assassination of President John F. Kennedy. Upon hearing the news I felt numb. The next thing I knew I was entering the base chapel. I don't know how so many soldiers got there so quickly, but there were men who were always prepared to fight to the death of us all standing and sitting there crying like babies. I never quite felt the same about Dallas although to that point it had been my favorite city on Earth. While in Germany, Velma and I took our much-delayed vacation in Paris, France. It made up for the honeymoon we never had.

All went well until some poor soul decided to end his life by jumping from the Eiffel Tower, unfortunately he landed on a touring American teacher, killing her as well.

My next permanent duty station was Fort Campbell, Kentucky. I loved being a "Screaming Eagle" but Clarksville, Tennessee was no Fayetteville, North Carolina, which added so much to being assigned to Fort Bragg, North Carolina. There I continued to grow as a young Non-Commissioned Officer and continues to work on my college courses. This would be the first of my back-to-back assignments to Fort Campbell.

During my assignment there I met many great soldiers and picked a few of them as friends. The best friends there were Sergeants Lloyd Oliver and Tony Salter. We were all family men who frequently got together for happy hour on Friday evenings or weekend cookouts at each other's homes. Lloyd encouraged me to apply for Jumpmaster School, which I did and enjoyed the course and being Jumpmaster on many jumps. I also had an opportunity to observe my three wonderful kids grow and mature under the leadership of their mother who spent far too much time worrying about me jumping out of perfectly good airplanes and hated the five mile runs we occasionally did as a unit on base.

There was much sadness around Fort Campbell because of the First Brigade's presence in Vietnam. It seemed that every day several families were notified that their Paratrooper had died in the war and the rest of us knew that it would only be a matter of time before we too would be in combat.

I left Fort Campbell, Kentucky in October 1966 for my second assignment to Aberdeen Proving Grounds, Maryland. This time it was to attend Officer Candidate School. My family moved back to McKinney for those six months. I took twenty-five sets of fatigues and three pairs of Corcoran jump boots with me to Aberdeen and believe me, they all came in handy. The trick was to keep one pair of boots on display under your bunk, one pair in the shoe shine shop, and one pair on your feet. If I had time I changed fatigues and boots after lunch each day. During my first weeks I was appointed Company Commander. I probably slept only about three hours per night because I wanted to set high standards for everyone who followed and it worked. We had a great class of Cadet leaders.

Our Cadre consisted of a Company Commander and two Tactical Officers. We had absolutely no contact with the rest of the Company Staff. The Company Commander was Captain Frederick Gorham. My Tactical Officer was Lieutenant Tom Everhart. They kept us on the run for six months.

During my second week there I was voted Class President, which proved quite challenging since I was the only black in my class. The greatest challenge was to face the Manager of the Aberdeen Maryland Theater, who wanted to run a segregated movie house. After I met with him and promised to ask the Base Commander to put the place off limits he saw things our way. You see, my white classmates had no desire to attend a segregated movie house while black and white soldiers were dying for this country every day in Vietnam.

I had a unique roommate in OCS. When Lieutenant Tom Everhart brought him to me and said "Marks is a little rich boy who comes from a wealthy family. He needs to get through this course. Show him the ropes. Teach him how to spit shine his side of the floor, make his bunk good and tight and keep his wall locker and footlocker straight and the rest is up to him. At that point," I became one Candidate with the workload of two. He took care of me too, when it was time to meet the taxicab at night and pick up our order of snacks a.k.a. Pogey Bait, usually hoagies, sodas, and candy bars. He went to collect the money from everyone, went with one other Candidate and picked up our late night snacks labeled by the Tactical Officers as Pogey Bait. The evening meal simply wasn't enough for a group of guys who ran everywhere they had to go. The one time he didn't perform my Pogey Bait run for me and I had to do it myself, Lieutenant Everhart was surprisingly in the car with the taxi driver who made the delivery. After being chewed out and doing countless push ups, we were forced to eat our food in the shower with the showers running, of course, which made a mess of everything and in addition to the cleaning the two of us who brought the trash can filled with food into the barracks had to execute additional push ups for letting our platoon down by getting caught.

Before we knew it the eighteenth week was approaching and we started preparing for our Pass in Review and Military Ball. We invited nurses from John Hopkins School of Nursing for the single guys, married candidates invited their wives, unaccompanied candidates were told to either dance with each other or stand there and watch. We chose the latter. When the list of names was posted candidates picked their dates. The fun part was when Jack Van Ashe saw the name Dawn and went absolutely berserk. "I have never known a girl named Dawn who wasn't simply gorgeous." Said Jack. He and a couple of our classmates ended up flipping coins for Dawn. Jack won.

I was tapped to be Commander of Troops for the 18th week Command review. It felt great being out front wearing three diamonds on my collar. We nailed it, the Adjutant, the

Color Guard, the Unit Commanders all looked great. And finally time came for us to meet the bus and our guests from John Hopkins. Jack Van Ashe was standing up front when Dawn and Jack met each other. We were all checking her out to see if she was what he had hoped for. She wasn't a Halle Berry, but she was fun to be around, and had great people skills. Jack couldn't wait for graduation because he got tired of being asked if he had heard from Dawn.

On 10 May 1967 we graduated and were Commissioned Second Lieutenants and headed our separate ways. I went back to the 101st Airborne Division, Fort Campbell, Kentucky but as a Lieutenant a few pay grades higher than the Staff Sergeant I had been when I left there. This was clearly a life changing experience for the entire family we moved into the Officer's housing area near the Country Club.

Velma, a nurse, had tried to get hired at the Clarksville Hospital when we were there before, but to no avail. Miraculously when I returned as an officer she was hired on the first try and her nursing director invited me to lunch. In addition to my old friends still at Campbell I now had a new set of friends and co-workers. Before leaving for OCS I planted the first hand salute on Warrant Officer Robert Brandenberg when he was appointed, I agreed to give it back if I returned to Campbell and he gave me my first salute there although he was no longer an NCO, which he and I both agreed was the backbone of the Army. We made that happen and he promised to frame the silver dollar.

My new job was Second Forward Support Platoon Leader. My platoon was assigned to the Second Brigade 101st Airborne Division. The 801st Maintenance Battalion had three such platoons. One assigned to each of the

Divisions Organic Brigades. My job was to advise the Brigade Commander on maintenance matters, lead the platoon and manage its resources. Being an Airborne Division we didn't have much heavy equipment to maintain, but certain important pieces had priority such as crew served weapons, sights and other instruments and the counter mortar radar computers and generators.

My stay at Fort Campbell, Kentucky as an Officer was short lived. While there I made new friends among the Junior Officer ranks and a few Senior Officers as well. Among the Junior Officers were Lieutenants Gerry Thames, Craig King, and Mel Starks. I also reunited with Robert Myers who was with me at Aberdeen, class #5-67. He was also picked to be a Forward Support Platoon Leader. Myers was the only red headed Lieutenant in the Battalion. We spent much time together, jumping out of the relatively new C141 jets, preparing for combat operations, and just being Lieutenants. Happy hour at the Officers Club quickly became our favorite weekend thing to do. Our favorite song was Brown Eyed Girl.

Of the Captain and aboves our favorites were Major Kells, Captain Ashbury, and our Company Commander Captain Brown. Chief Warrant Officer John Meadows was the one Warrant Officer who mattered the most to us. All of our NCO's were special. None more special than SFC Paul Black, my platoon sergeant and sergeants Florian Zahn and Dan Clay. They took good care of us newbies, as we were called. After we were at Campbell a couple of months all hell broke loose. A new Commanding General took over the 101st. During certain times of the day we couldn't drive our cars on base. We had to be in military vehicles or on foot.

On a very calm day we received a message that changed our lives. All officers were told to report to the base theater at 1300 hours (1 pm). When we arrived we noticed the Commanding General and members of his staff were sitting on the stage and their uniforms were different from ours. The Commanding General, Major General Barsanti, told us that he had summoned us there to tell us that the Commander in Chief of the Armed Forces had selected the Second and Third Brigades of the 101st Airborne Division for duty in South Vietnam to help the people there maintain the right to choose their own destiny and that over the course of the next several months we would prepare our units for deployment.

When we were finished training for war we took our families' home to prepare for deployment. For me that meant going back home to McKinney, Texas and finding a place for the wife and kids to live. As it turned out the Johnson family estate, which consisted of three houses had one unoccupied house. It was the house that Velma's grandparents on her father's side had lived in. She decided to spend the year that I was in Nam there since it was so close to her parents.

I had two weeks to get them settled in before returning to Fort Campbell. The house was a modest three-bedroom home with one bathroom and two formals. That meant the boys would share a room, Harriett would have a room, and their mom would take the master bedroom. While there, my job was to paint the rooms and put down new rugs, which provided the two high points of my two weeks at home. The first being the 19th Century Silver Dollar I found under the linoleum rug when I removed it to put down the carpet. Velma pledged to keep it forever since it probably belonged to her grandparents. The second was when I decided to paint Harriett's room. As I was completing the job she asked me to get some of the blue paint that I had used to paint John and Christopher's room. I asked what for and she wouldn't tell me. After I poured the paint in the pan she started looking sad, then she dropped the bomb on me. She said "The boys, you, and I are going to put our hand in the paint and put them on the wall, so we will always have them together in case you don't come back." That broke my heart while at the same time made me realize my not coming home from Vietnam was not an option.

A few days later we loaded into our little Chevy Corvair (a different one) and headed to Dallas Love Field for my return flight to Fort Campbell, Kentucky. Upon arrival I was told that I was the OIC on flight F077 from Fort Campbell to Bien Hoa, South Vietnam and that I would have some members of my platoon, a medical doctor and three medics assigned to my flight, also a pallet of ammunition, a pallet of water, a pallet of rations, a ¾ ton vehicle, a Jeep, and a 105mm Howitzer that would double as a maintenance float and base camp defense, equipped with Bee Hive rounds in my sector of the perimeter where ever I was stationed in country.

Before I knew it 16 December 1967 rolled around and I found myself all alone in a crowd at Fort Campbell Army Airfield preparing to ship out. My thought of the future where frequently interrupted by thoughts of a past that had gone by much too fast.

I took the time to think of my early childhood the good times, the hard times and how great it would be to have my father, my number one fan here cheering for me as I prepared for the biggest game of my life. The good guys vs. the bad guys where the winner takes all. My most intimate thoughts took me to the sidelines of the McKinney Football Stadium where as a member of the Doty High School Bobcats, I stood with the rest of the team on a Friday night clinching my helmet honoring our National Anthem, and waiting for the final note so we could take the field and give it our all. The feeling was the same. The chills up and down our spine, the will to win, but this time it was all different. We held our helmets but on this day we weren't even at Campbell Army Airfield to make our usual exit from a C141 jet at 1250 feet. We were there to fly to the other side of the world to engage in combat operations. After a short pep talk to my platoon which ended with the usual "Hip hip hurray" we reported to our respective planes, slowly taxied out to the runway and in a few minutes as the giant aircraft lifted off let out the loudest "Lets go get em!" yell you have ever heard. We were off to Vietnam with three scheduled refueling stops in between. I took time to study the expressions on each man's face and said a little prayer for each of them. I actually thought God would grant my wish for each of them to return home alive. After all he had given me the touchdown I prayed for, and the sons and daughter to carry on the bloodline.

The people were great at all stops they had food, hugs, and waved the US Flags. We were all quite proud to be Americans and grateful to the people of Guam and the Philippines. I don't think the people near the Air Base in California knew members of the Second and Third Brigades 101st Airborne would be making a pit stop in their state. On Flight F077 that day were Captain Doctor Sam Oberlander,

Staff Sergeant Benny Swint, Specialist Six Johnny Mayes, Sergeant Florian Zahn, Specialist Five Edward Durham, Specialist Four John Pride, Specialist Four James Herich, Specialist Four Charles Cutlerrez, Specialist Four Michael Herrera, Private First Class Russell Milberry, Private First Class Donnell Sain, Private First Class Lewis Boncy, Private First Class James Webb and yours truly. Some were members of my platoon others were members of a task force put together for deployment purposes. By the month of May three would have been killed and three would have been wounded. The rest of my 42-man unit who were on two other C141s with equipment would fair a little better. Not too long after taking off from Clark Air Force Base the pilot came on the address system and told us Bien Hoa was under rocket attack, we should lock and load and put our weapons on safe. We were also told the planes would not be stopping, that the Air Force crew would attach pilot chutes to the pellets and my drivers would drive the vehicles off as the plane moves down the run way. Once on the ground the objective was to get the vehicles and pellets off the runway as quickly as possible so other planes could execute as we had. We did that and assumed the prone position around our equipment until the rocket attack ended and the all clear was given.

About an hour and twenty minutes later a voice said "All clear, empty your weapons, put them on safe, and follow me in a straight file." Little did we know the worse was yet to come. As we followed the tall lean Major to a huge warehouse looking building for our in country orientation, our attention was drawn to what seemed to be little airport tractors with narrow luggage trailers hitched to them, but these trailers were carrying very special cargo, the remains of fallen comrades. You could have heard a grain of sand hit the ground. The silence was broken by a young voice behind me who said, "I don't want to go like that. I don't want to go like that." That's when I told my first lie. I said, "Don't worry. You won't. One year from today we are all going to meet back here and climb aboard a big bird and go home." I had two choices, say something similar to what I said or say nothing.

At the in country orientation we were welcomed to Viet Nam and told the 25th Infantry Division located at Cu-Chi would be our in country host unit and we would join them at Cu-Chi and train with them for approximately one month before occupying our own LZ (Landing Zone) which was the size base camp for most Brigades in the war zone. After the briefing we loaded on to our vehicles and convoyed to Cu-Chi with individual and crew served weapons locked and loaded. While traveling to Cu-Chi we heard a few shots in a distance but didn't return fire because we couldn't see who we were shooting at and had not been given the go ahead to recon by fire. The next morning when we inspected our equipment we found bullet holes in our signal van and in a few vehicles.

Although we had trained for driving under blackout conditions, the variables of uncertainty and threat of being attacked as we drove lay heavy on our minds. We spent the first full day at Cu-Chi setting up tents, filling sand bags and building fighting positions. This went on for about a week and then it was time for us to start in country training in and around Cu-Chi and the rubber plantations. Unknown to us we had to be in I Corps by the end of January.

During our stay at Cu-Chi we participated in our first field exercise as a unit, it was executed on a Rubber Plantation about 100 miles from Cu-Chi. During that exercise we had a Huey crash and lost everyone on board and a 105 mm round "cook off" that took two lives. At the end of the exercise I was selected to be convoy commander. I contacted a Military Police Lieutenant by the name of Boy and asked him to make sure we had air cover for the approximately 100 mile trip back to Cu-Chi. We had our air cover and all went well. Upon returning to Cu-Chi one of our bunkers took a direct hit. We lost the crew but found a city under a city. As it turned out the NVA and Viet Cong had tunneled under the base at Cu-Chi and built underground quarters and a hospital. The healthy were captured; the wounded were admitted to the field hospital at Cu-Chi. My platoon and I visited that hospital during the 1967 Christmas holidays and adopted a little Vietnamese as our own personal patient. We even checked on her after leaving for I corps. She did survive her injuries.

Chapter Five

TET Offensive And The War Thereafter

On 29 January 1968 we found ourselves at the Bien Hoa Airport for our trip to I Corps in preparation for the TET Offensive. For our trip from Bien Hoa to Hue Phu Bai we boarded C130's the workhorse of the US Air Force. It seems that we got there much too soon. We landed at Phu Bai and set up our headquarters in a large cemetery. Because of the number of head wounds caused by fragments we were encouraged to sleep with out heads up next to the grave headstones for safety. A couple of the troops expressed concern about sleeping on top of graves, I convinced them that it wasn't the dead we had to worry about. After a couple of days they agreed with me.

My first concern was the hill a couple of miles from my platoons side of the perimeter. I was told not to worry about it; we would only be there a couple of days. The couple of days ended up being over a week because of bad weather and the fact that the North Vietnamese and Viet Cong had blown the bridge near the City of Hue along highway 1 that we needed to travel to get to the Second Brigade base camp Landing Zone Jane just south of the DMZ. During our stay at what would become Camp Eagle, headquarters for the 101st Airborne Division in Viet Nam. We were joined by members of the 82nd Airborne Division, my old unit. I had not seen so many Paratroopers at one place since President Kennedy came to visit the 82nd at Pope Air Force Base in the early sixties. And I had never seen so many black Paratroopers.

The huge buildup of forces in late 1967 and early January 1968 included the 2nd and 3rd Brigade 101st Airborne Division, 3rd Brigade 82nd Airborne Division, 1st Brigade 5th Infantry Division and some of the 40,000 soldiers called up from Reserve Units which was short of General Westmoreland's request to President Johnson, but still equaled more than 3 ½ Divisions. With that knowledge our leadership in Viet Nam decided to put a large portion of the combat forces in I Corps, which extended from the vicinity of Dak To to the DMZ. When we arrived in I Corps, we first flew into Phu Bai which would become Camp Eagle Headquarters 101st Airborne Division, with the 2nd Brigade first moving to LZ Jane near Dong Ha with the HQ of the First Air Calvary Division already occupying Camp Evans near Quang Tri we made up a formidable fighting force. As the TET Offensive slowed down a bit the 2nd Brigade 101st Airborne Division, which we were a part of, set up a permanent base called Landing Zone Sally just south of Camp Evans, about 35 miles north of Hue. LZ Sally would remain the home of Second Forward Support Platoon. From there we supported all of the brigade units fire support bases in addition to LZ Sally. QL 1 or Street Without Joy, a source of anguish and hardship for all whose misfortunes required them to travel it was our main supply route.

During that period, I saw former members of the 8th Infantry Division boxing team that I had known in Germany in 1963-1965 including Carlton Brooks and Gene Jefferson, both Sergeants by now who had been two of the best fighters on the team. I had hoped they would have left the Army and turned pro but like me they enjoyed being Paratroopers too much to do that, the Army proved to be the best thing to have happened to many of us.

One of our greatest Infantry Commanders was Lieutenant Colonel Bishop, Commander of 1st 501st Battalion, 101st Airborne Division. Behind his back, many of us Junior Officers referred to him as Mother Bishop, because he cared so much for us. He always had time to stop and talk to us and ask if we were writing home, being paid properly, and looking out for our troops. It seems that us company grade officers were not the only ones impressed by the Colonel. The men and women civilians at Fort Campbell cared so much for him that they built him an Outhouse with a commode seat, paper roller, and half moon on the door. It traveled with us from Campbell to Bien Hoa, to Cu Chi, and to Phu Bai. During one of our daily rocket attack harassment sessions, which included artillery airbursts, that drove us all under anything high enough to crawl under, I heard troops applauding during the attack. As it turned out, Colonel Bishop's outhouse had taken a direct hit and was no more. I was later told that his troops built him another one but I was never privileged to see or sneak into it.

Other memorable events associated with the outbreak of TET included my being told to keep a good head count of my troops and make sure noise and blackout regulations were carried out. On this particular edgy Phu Bai night I heard the voice of one of the younger troops singing one of the Temptations favorites, My Girl. I eased out of my sleeping bag to encourage him to tone it down since Charlie could hear him giving away our position. His reply was "Sir, the sound of generators, the huge tents and antennas do a pretty good job of that." I agreed with him but ordered him to shut up anyway. As I returned to my sleeping bag I saw a soldier standing near it with a stick in his hands. He asked, "Sir were you sleeping here?" My reply was "Yes. Why?" He said, "As I was passing by I noticed movement coming up out of the cracked ground near the headstone and it was this bamboo viper. He's dead now. Had you been in your sleeping bag you might be too." I shined my flashlight into the crack and didn't see anything. I took my entrenching tool and put dirt in the crack then ordered the rest of my troops to do the same. Then I joined the troops and we softly sang My Girl, Brown Eyed Girl, and I Wanna Go Home. Sleep was out of the question for me. I didn't like snakes and rightfully so, the troops were weary of incoming rockets.

The next night proved to be much worse than the night before. It was the night of 31 January 1968 when PFC Russell Milberry and other troops thought sleeping in a huge tent with a big white cross on it was safer than sleeping in the troop area. None of us realized how little respect the Viet Cong and NVA had for the Geneva Convention, but we would soon find out, the big hospital tent took direct hits from 122 MM rockets and Russell became the first fatality of flight F077 and we had barely been in country one month. Although we had witnessed several fatalities this was personal. The troops knew Russell and although fighting as infantrymen was their secondary specialties they were ready for revenge. When we were told we would be moving to Landing Zone Jane just south of the DMZ they all wanted to be part of the advance party, so that could occupy five man fighting positions in our sector as part of base camp defense.

One of the most disturbing things to happen to me while at Hue Phu Bai during the 1968 TET Offensive was when a young paratrooper came to me and said "Sir, I need to talk to someone." My first question was "Have you talked to your platoon sergeant?" and he said "Yes and the platoon leader too." I said, "I will be glad to listen but remember I'm not in your unit and may not be able to help you." His replay was "Yes sir. I understand." He went on to tell me he had a dream that if he went on the next mission with his company he would be killed. He then said "Sir, I have a wife and baby back in the world and I really want to return home to them. But it's just this one mission. This one mission has my number." I spoke to the Chaplain, the red cross representative and an officer from his unit who said what I already knew. If you allow one soldier to stay back because he thinks he's going to die where would it end? He could stay here and get killed by a rocket. The soldier went on that operation and came back in a body bag. All I could do was have a serious conversation with God as I had done many times before in my life.

Within three days we were all air lifted to Jane, our equipment was airlifted by crane helicopters. I would like to have gotten my hands on the guy who told me to pop smoke and stand there and guide the chopper in. It literally blew me about 25 yards away. My first combat bruises but not my last.

The order of the day at Jane was to attend an early morning briefing by the Second Brigade Commander Colonel John Cushman then return to our units and execute the mission for the day. The rocket attacks on LZ Jane were deadly. We lost several Second Brigade members the first few days. Captain Caldwell of Headquarters Company was one of the first. They hit us while we were still digging in and filling our sandbags. My Jeep took a direct hit. The only reason I wasn't under it when it was hit was because I couldn't beat the rocket to it.

As the dust settled Specialist Heit, Specialist Williams, Specialist Apodaca, and Specialist Voss were running as fast as they could to get to our designated platoon headquarters area because they felt quite sure those of us in that area had been hit. That's how close we came to being taken out. The 122-millimeter rocket was a strange bird. The enemy just pointed it toward our base camp and fired and accepted whatever they could get. Unfortunately for us they were lucky more often than not. During that one short session they took out several vehicles, several bunkers, and killed and injured some of our troops. Most of the officers who were not out on operations or fire support bases went to the morgue tent to see Captain Caldwell before his remains were shipped back to the rear. He commanded that type of respect. After a few weeks at LZ Jane we were ordered to set up a permanent LZ just south of Camp Evans and north of the city of Hue along highway 1, better known as the street without joy. This time I wasn't picked to be convoy commander and my platoons movement order placed us almost last in the convoy, which meant we would still be on the road when nightfall arrived. However we were not the least bit worried because counting our maintenance float 40MM grenade launchers, M60 machine guns we were as heavily armed as an Airborne Infantry platoon. We had received orders to recon by fire if provoked and we had much more than our basic load of ammunition, which meant recon by fire was not a problem.

The second forward support platoon closed in at our new base camp, Landing Zone Sally at around 17:45 hours. My next order was to assemble a recovery team and retrieve a 2-½ ton truck loaded with Claymore mines, grenades, and light anti tank weapons (LAWS) that had broken down in unsecured territory because we couldn't allow those weapons to be taken by the Viet Cong or NVA. If left there overnight that would surely be the case. As we recovered the equipment along with the two soldiers left there to guard it we drove through likely ambush sites. On my command two M60 machine guns, two 40mm grenade launchers gave our rendition of a mad minute as we reconned by fire to prevent possible ambush when passing likely ambush sites. The Second Brigade grunts looked at our troops differently from then on, especially the two who had been left there to guard the vehicle. We pulled into LZ Sally to the cheers of the MPs on the gate and the troops in the bunkers near the gate. The Brigade Commander was so elated that we kept the Munitions out of Charlie's hands that he passed word down to me to put the recovery team in for the Arcom with "V" device which I gladly did as soon as I could get my little ole manual typewriter out of moth balls. The next day was business as usual for me as I found myself once again on a helicopter heading to a fire support bases to deliver 105 MM Howitzer sights to units that had broken one or more as the weapons were being hoisted out by helicopters.

By now things began to get better in terms of operations. Sergeant Paul Black, the Platoon Sergeant for the Second Platoon and Sergeant Thomas Good began to take charge of internal operations, as I knew they would. Manning perimeter defense was their baby. Using 105 mm Ammo Boxes the five man bunkers we built began to look like underground houses. The idea was to provide as much comfort as we could for the young Paratroopers who would spend fifty percent of their time in those bunkers. Each bunker had at least one wooden wall and a floor. Their furniture included sleeping bags, air mattresses, one lantern, one field table, one chair and an S & P Packet filled with Pogey Bait. The ground level of the bunkers had a floor, a top and three fighting positions. Many parts of the bombed out railroads were used in constructing our bunkers. The billeting area where the troops who were not on duty slept were tin topped screened in hooches built by the Sea Beas, they were equipped with wooden cots and footlockers and an occasional piece of furniture built out of ammunition boxes. I slept in a hex tent about halfway between the row of Hooches and my assigned fighting positions. LZ Sally would be home for at least ten more months and our duties would be combat support by day and combat arms by night and it would be the same for all combat support and service support troops assigned to the Second Brigade 101st Airborne Division with the exception of medics and chaplain staff personnel.

Our day jobs were easy because our troops had fared well in MOS training and most had a couple of years experience on the job. Our E-5s and above were unbeatable. I started out by returning from the Brigade Commanders early morning meetings and passing on the pertinent information so they too understood what the Brigade Commander expected from each assigned unit. He always reminded us to be the best we could be when on perimeter defense duty, because everyone inside was depending on us to be the first line of defense, and sound the alarm should the base get attacked. Officers and Senior NCOs were required to perform perimeter OIC and NCOIC duty for the perimeter that meant during our tour of duty that night we were required to walk the perimeter and check the troops on duty at each bunker in our assigned sector and beyond. In doing so we check out their weapons, ammo, water, snacks, and any concerns they might have. On one particular night as I approach a bunker I noticed cigarette lights on the top of the bunker I was approaching, we exchanged the challenge and password and I told them I saw their cigarette lights from 50 yards and the Viet Cong could see them from a much further distance and they were subjecting themselves to sniper fire. The look on their faces said either they didn't believe me or they didn't think they had to listen to me. As I departed for the bunker to their left I looked back and they were smoking again. Since I only had one more bunker to check before reaching the end of my sector I kept going as I turned around and headed back I heard a familiar sound, it was the sound of a 10mm mortar round leaving the tube. I started running and screaming for them to get into their bunker but the mortar round was faster than I was. After about my fifth step I heard the earth shaking sound of SHUMB! SHUMB! and our troops in the bunkers on both sides of the smokers opening up with several bursts of M60 machine gun fire in the direction of the flashes they had seen when the mortars were fired. As I reached the bunker the troops who were in the bottom of the bunker waiting their term to pull watch had reached the two injured troops each had several shrapnel holes in some part of their bodies. One looked at me and said, "I'm sorry sir." The other was moaning in pain. I stayed there until the medics arrived, filled out a report and made sure replacements arrived at that bunker. I never saw those two again, but was assured that they had been recommended for Purple Hearts for their injuries and hoped they had learned a valuable lesson. The next evening I called the entire platoon together and used that incident as a lesson learned, although I performed perimeter duty two or three times per week I never saw another trooper sitting on a bunker smoking.

In early March the TET aftermath was beginning to settle in. I was called on to a take a crew to Fire Support Base to work on 81MM mortars. The Huey dropped us off, the troops performed their duties and we waited for hours to be picked up. Being at a fire support base meant the noise level was at a new decimal. The 105 MM Howitzers seldom stopped firing during our stay there. As we returned from my side of the Huey I observed a LOCH helicopter crash in what seemed to be slow motion. When the rotor blade disintegrated it seemed that pieces were hurled as high as 100 feet in the air as the fuselage began rolling end over end the tail section, tail rotor and doors broke away from the doomed chopper. To my surprise there were no fatalities in what surely seemed to be a loss of life situation. All of us, who frequently flew in order to accomplish our missions, began saying, "If I have to be on a helicopter that crashes let it be a loch. With those strong roller bars on each side of the fuselage." As I began to settle into my job as a platoon leader in combat I became more and more concerned about those around me. I spent more time inspecting my sector of the perimeter to insure it met doctrines guidelines for an appropriate forward edge of the battle area (FEBA) and spending quality time with each member of the platoon to make sure their pay was right, making sure they were going to the mess hall to eat and not trying to live off junk food, making sure they were writing home and receiving mail in return. Because of rocket attacks some troops didn't like to be part of large gatherings and stayed away from mess halls. I also checked weapons and ammunition weekly while NCO's checked them daily. As we settled down at LZ Sally I was able to visit and receive visits from my friends Lieutenant Lee Grimsley from Tuskegee Institute stopped by, Lieutenants Gary A. Scott and Michael L. Gandy stopped by to say hello. We often traded goodies from home. They all loved my peanut butter cookies and I enjoyed their variety of candy bars. About once a month I traveled south to Camp Eagle to visit headquarters where

I was privileged to see Captain Tom Everhart, one of my tactical officers from OCS, Lieutenant Thames, Lieutenant King, Lieutenant Starks, Captain Asbury, and meet with LTC Danny Benefiel, our Battalion Commander. Those trips were usually combined with a Post Exchange visit to purchase goodies for the troops. On one such trip I remember driving around a big pile of dirt in the middle of highway 1. As we drove around it my driver, Specialist Heit asked, "Why is that big pile of dirt in the middle of highway 1?" Without hesitation I replied, "It's probably covering a body." We looked at each other and kept driving. On our return trip, we looked at that point again as we approached it. We closed in to LZ Sally slightly before dark, ate and reported to our sector and waited for the inevitable rocket attack.

The next few weeks found Specialist Heit and me making more and more road trips as Highway One became more secure. On one March morning as we drove between LZ Sally and Camp Evans we heard small arms fire coming from our left front, at the same time we noticed a 2 ½ ton truck to our front, flip over. There were no other vehicles in sight as we pulled over. The driver was running around the vehicle saying "We took fire from those bushes sir, we took fire from those bushes!" I got on the radio and reported the incident. After hearing the voice of Lieutenant Colonel Julius Becton, I felt that all would be well. As we looked in the cab of the truck, we noticed a dead courier with a briefcase strapped to his arm. We stayed on the scene until Military Police arrived.

The end of TET Offensive and the War thereafter in March brought on April showers for me personally, because of the toll the war took on my friends. On 30 March 1968, while enroute to Camp Evans to pick up a sight for a 105 MM Howitzer, I decided to stop by the old burned out school near the bridge that crossed the Bô river where Lieutenants Scott and Gandy were located to drop off some of my fresh batch of peanut butter cookies I had just received from home. When I stepped onto the porch, the Company First Sergeant who was sitting by the door greeted me. He asked if he could help me. I told him I was there to drop off cookies to my friends Scott and Gandy. He looked at me with a blank stare and said, "They are both dead, killed last night in an ambush along with Lieutenant Rodriguez." My body went numb; what a sacrifice, I thought; an All-American sacrifice. Lieutenant Scott was an African American from New York, Lieutenant Gandy was a Caucasian from Kansas and Lieutenant Rodriguez, a Hispanic from Hawaii; all full of life and just 23 years old. I had the reasons; three of them to be exact, I just needed an opportunity to shoot an NVA or Viet Cong. Maybe three would be better. From then on each time I passed that old school building I had flashbacks, which were painful, after that I arranged for more helicopter rides to points north of Landing Zone Sally. My final road trip to Camp Evans was to see several members of my platoon who had been poisoned by drinking water from a pond that had been purified by our water purification unit - they were back to duty within three days. April did not start out too good either because some sick-minded hater thought killing Dr. Martin Luther King, Jr. would halt progress but it would not.

April and May were usual months filled with visits to fire support bases, Camp Evans and Camp Eagle. And ground attacks on Landing Zones, which were usually Brigade Headquarters sites. Just as Camps were Division Headquarters sites increased drastically during one such attack we lost one of the sharpest young Sergeants in the 101st Airborne Division, Sergeant Florian Zahn who was my

Non-Commissioned Officer in Charge on Flight FO77, at that point I just wanted to give up. About a month later things got ever worse with the loss of Senator Robert F. Kennedy. I was particularly shaken because I had written him a letter telling him I did not think the country was ready for another Kennedy and it would be a dangerous thing to do, but failed to mail it. After his death I was encouraged to send it to magazines posthumously; I did and it was published.

It was not long before it was time for my good friend Lieutenant Mel Starks and me to fly to Hawaii to meet Velma and Pat. We arrived there on 19 June 1968. We stayed a week; ate great food and mixed with people who were protesting in the streets but appreciated men and women in uniform. When we visited Pearl Harbor everything about our little war was put into proper perspectives, our war was hell, but it was peanuts compared to WWII where so many lives were lost for freedoms we would have never known. As I stood there looking at the battle sites I got the same numb feeling I felt upon learning of Scott, Gandy and Rodriguez, only this time my pain was for the loss of over two thousand. As we left Honolulu on our return flight to Nam, we watched our wives as the pilot banked the plane until they were simply little dots on the ground. About a month after returning to Sally, my unit was upgraded to company size, meaning a captain would be sent to command it. I requested and received permission to remain that position in what was referred to as the Forward Area until after the Command Inspection, which gave me about three months command time at company level in combat. On 4 August 1968 we had a very serious grenade attack that threatened Landing Zone Sally, which also involved Charlie Company. That incident could have ended life for several of us and gave me many reasons to look forward to spending my last three months in Vietnam at Camp Eagle, a large more secure place to be; little did I know an ambush patrol awaited me upon assignment to Camp Eagle. On my final road trip from LZ Sally to Camp Eagle as we approached the pile of dirt that we observed upon our first road trip to Camp Eagle almost a year earlier, we noticed the road repair crew had reached that point. Under that pile of dirt was a South Vietnamese Officer and the motorcycle he was riding when he died. Upon receiving reports of movement in front of our sector of the perimeter at Camp Eagle, Lieutenant Colonel Benefiel decided to send out a patrol to set up a "L" shaped ambush six hundred meters in front of Sector A, Camp Eagle. Lasting seven hours into the night, a Viet Cong ground transport Unit walked into our patrol. Our eleven-man ambush patrol captured 112 detainees and returned them to base for G2 interrogation but not before engaging in hand to hand combat with a few of them. A young Sergeant Rath was simply outstanding as the Non-Commissioned Officer in charge of the patrol. My youngest, Christopher, would have had a horrible birthday had things gone wrong for me. This was the second time the number one hundred and twelve (112) had played a part in my life; the first was during a football game.

On 13 December 1968, I made my final entry into my diary and boarded a big Pan American Jet for "The World." As we boarded the plane I looked around and did not see a soul that I had ever seen before – every face was "new" to me. This wonderful Stewardess (as they were called then), who was so beautiful I thought immediately of the movie star, Natalie Wood. This angel of the airways walked up to me, handed me a cool damp towel and said, "Welcome Aboard Paratrooper – let us take you home!"

As I looked around a few soldiers were shouting and a few shed tears of joy, others tears of sorrow for the friends they left behind. As I look out of my window, I could see columns of vehicles heading towards the Vietnam Delta on a seemingly endless highway, and at a distance I could see Navy or Air force Jets diving and releasing their ordinance as the rising sun danced off of their fuselages. "That's the way to go!" I thought. I wondered if one could be Robert Atkinson, my childhood friend from Drew. Should I ever return to this place, it will be as an Aviator. I put my headset on and listened to Diana Ross and the Supremes sing "Put Yourself In My Place" and fell asleep and slept all the way to the other side of the world.

CHAPTER SIX

Challenge In Action

HAVING FLOWN OUT TO THE USS Sanctuary and successfully passing my flight physical prior to leaving Vietnam in 1968, my stay at Fort Bragg's 12th Support Brigade was simply a brief stop over en route to Flight School as soon as I could make it happen. As it turned out getting a class assignment would take me about a year and a half in the mean time I took advantage of my stay at Bragg by continuing my studies toward my degree and after reading a story about Astronaut John Glenn, which said he felt it was necessary to take private flying lessons before attending military flight training, my thought was what's good for a great aviator like Astronaut Glenn has to be good for me. My next step was to join the Fort Bragg Flying Club. My first flight was on 25 February 1969 in a 100 horse power Cessna 150, Certificate Number 2641J. I soloed after 14 hours of flying time and flew a total of 45 minutes without my instructor being on board. When he told me to taxi over to the side and to let him out of the plane my level of joy was overwhelming and oh how I wished my father could have been there to see me. This small segment of my flight training would come in handy later as an Officer Student Pilot at Ft. Stewart, Georgia.

My stay at Fort Bragg was an enjoyable one. My boss while I was there was Colonel Henry Emmerson who was better known as the "Gun Fighter". While there I was given command of the Command Maintenance Readiness Assistance Team. Our job was to go out and give units assistance visits and then at a later date make an unannounced visit and conduct a surprise inspection that was designed to measure a units mission readiness so when the CMI or IG Team came around all 12th Support Brigade unites would be ready for inspection.

While in that position, I was assisted by a Chief Warrant Officer and several great non-commissioned officers. One of the NCOs was Sergeant First Class Henry Winston whom I would meet later on in life in Natchez, Mississippi. In May of 1969 I was promoted to Captain, the problem with that was being 28 years old and still looking 22 required me to be serious at all times in order to get the respect I deserved from some of the Junior NCO's whose excuses included not seeing the Captain bars on my collar or on my cap. Old excuse, wrong Captain. I often replied by saying well in that case I guess you didn't notice the Screaming Eagle on my right shoulder either, referring to the fact that I had served in combat with the 101st Airborne Division, however there were even more young Sergeants who looked forward to saluting me. Some I had been privileged to serve with prior to attending Officer Candidate School. Sergeants Lloyd Oliver, Tony Salter and Ollie Miller, all exceptional Non-Commissioned Officers and dear friends of mine when I too wore Chevrons along with that group. I didn't have to worry about them respecting me as a Commissioned Officer any more than they had to worry about me respecting them as Non-Commissioned Officers. We were professionals. I would end up moving off base because the Officers wife next door who didn't like seeing cars in front of my quarters with red decals on them. Thanks to her I purchased my first home. It was a new split-level house in Fayetteville's North Hills sub-division. All ranks that could afford to purchase homes there lived there. I noticed no difference between the Enlisted, Warrants, Commissioned or Civilians. We were all proud American citizens, and that was all that mattered.

First Sergeant Hale and his family lived across the street from us and became life long friends. They looked after our property while we were in Georgia and Alabama attending the Officers Fixed Wing Aviators course. In addition to being Commander of the CMRAT Team, I worked in the plans office of the 12th Support Brigade the only negative thing about that assignment was that I was not in a jump slot for the first time in my Army career except while I was in Officer Candidate School.

Having been in the 82nd Airborne Division as a young soldier I understood the fact that I was in Airborne Country. Probably more so than any other place on earth, Fort Bragg was home to Green Berets the 82nd Airborne Division and the 18th Airborne Corps; enough high spirited "can do" attitudes to go around and to me that was all good. Of utmost importance to me was getting to flight school and back to Nam as an aviator before the war ended. Although I wouldn't dare let my family know the latter part. I seemed to be running into obstacle after obstacle. My physical had expired, I was required to take another Flight Aptitude Test, thanks to the course I took called General Aeronautics, I was prepared for most of the flight related questions and breathed through the FAST examination. After that it was simply the waiting game. While waiting I decided to organize an intermediate league football team. We called them the North Hills Raiders and it seemed that most of the neighborhood got behind those kids. They put North Hills on the map.

Coaching that team gave me as much personal satisfaction as anything I've ever done. My two sons, John III and Christopher, were too small to play but they helped me with the equipment and simply fell in love with football. I also took time to take the kids to many activities on Fort Bragg. The main attraction for them was Armed Forces Day where they got a chance to ride on vehicles; witness live fire exercises and see paratroopers from the 82nd Airborne Division jump on one of Fort Bragg's several Drop Zones. Having heard me talk about the day President Kennedy touched my shoulder and said you are a good looking Paratrooper, there was no way I could not take them to Pope Air Force Base. I just couldn't take them to the runway where we stood during his visit. They were kids at their best and said "Wow! President Kennedy was here!" Like me they were in Germany when he died and were quite young. Being lovers of sports I also took them to Fayetteville State Teachers College for football games. One day while hard at work in the Plans Division, I received a large brown envelope from headquarters; in it, was what I' had been waiting on for a very long time, orders for Flight School, Special Order Number 46 dated 5 March 1970. The orders actually assigned me to Fort Stewart and Fort Rucker Alabama, TDY enroute to South Vietnam, it was the latter part of the assignment orders that made whether or not to take the family with me to flight school a no-brainer.

I was so happy that day that I offered to take everyone to the "O Club" for Happy Hour. That all changed when one of the Staff Officers, Major Kowalski, said "I'll bet you a fifth of Scotch you won't make it to graduation, – about 15% don't make it you know!" Instead of replying I walked over, looked him in his eyes and gave him the strongest handshake I had ever given anyone. I called for a rain check on the Happy Hour and promised a fair well "Get Together" before departing for Fort Steward. Over the course of the next several weeks, I took more flying lessons and visited friends I thought I would never see again.

It wasn't easy to decide what to do with a new house that your wife simply loved so we agreed to keep it and she agreed to allow me to let a young hard working E-4 and his wife live in the house rent free while we were gone. I reported to Fort Stewart on 17 June 1970. My orders gave me the reporting date. Having been in the Army for almost eleven years by then, I knew how to report in properly which I did, however, the Officer handling the Orientation looked at me and said where have you been? I read the reporting time instructions from my orders so everyone could hear it and took a seat. He stared at me; J.W. Hendrix, whom I had not yet met, looked at me and said, "Tell him to go to hell!" I wanted to but didn't. We received our section assignments and were told that one week we would have academics in the morning and fly in the afternoon and switch over the next week. We were told that our class included Warrant Officer Candidates who had already completed Warrant Officer Candidate Training at Fort Walters Texas. That our primary training would be in a 213 horsepower Cessna 172, that our multi-engine training would be in the260 horsepower Beach Baron and that every student would undergo Tactical Training in a Tail Dragger, the 210 horsepower Cessna 01 Bird Dog and from there we could be transitioned into other Fixed Wing Aircraft and a few of us might even become dual rated and learn to fly helicopters later on in our careers. After in processing we were issued our flight gear. Getting my Flight Helmet was especially important to me, because if meant I was really there, what had seemed like a dream to that point suddenly seemed true. Unmarried members of our class and Warrant Officer Candidates lived on base, those of use who were accompanied by our spouses lived in nearby Trailer Courts in the vicinity of Fort Stewart Georgia, I rented a mobile home in Hinesville Georgia. Our first time in a mobile home; it took some getting used to for Velma and the kids to make the transition from living in luxury to the reduced living space our mobile home afforded us, though some of my classmates rented much nicer ones called double wides. The kids watched much television, especially Room 222, which they shared with their friends who were not permitted to watch that particular program in their homes. Room 222 was a black TV program, quite popular in 1970.

On our fist bus ride to the flight line we all got to know each other better. During that trip someone started speaking of their ties to the aviation industry and told how their fathers had been military pilots, airline pilots, and some had been in airport management. Finally one of my classmate said, "Jack what does your dad do?" I assumed he thought my Dad had been in aviation as well, I simply said my father was a tractor driver in Mississippi, and quiet came over the bus the look on J.W.'s face said this is the United States of America this is what we do. There are no limits on how far one can climb.

Primary Flight Training was all work; everything in the classroom was well organized and fast moving. The classes were taught by Doss Aviation, most of the instructors were former military with a few active duty instructors. Doss Aviation was organized like a military unit; the head person was our Fight Commander from Doss. All of the Doss Instructors word the OD Nomax Flight Suits; we wore the gray one-piece flight suits. My first flight took place on 24

June 1970. My plane was the T41 Tail number 15086, 213 horsepower, much more powerful than the 100 horsepower Cessna 150 I had flown at Fort Bragg.

My first test of my flying skills was a progress check ride that we all received on the same day given by a Military Flight Examiner it was designed to check both student performance and the performance of the Doss Aviation Instructor. I was first to go that morning. The Captain I flew with was a beady eyed Infantry Officer who was to the point on every maneuver as he well should have been. Happily I passed and all was well for a while. On 13 July 1970 I took my first solo check ride. My instructor lived up to the temper of the times by saying he had never soloed a black student and didn't intend to start by soloing me. Although I could not believe he was saying that to a US Army Captain three times decorated for heroism. I elected to ride with him anyway, hoping I would be the first. I failed, either because I wasn't good enough or because of his convictions. Not because I had failed but because of his comments before we even left the ground, and because I knew I had already soloed at Bragg I requested and received permission to visit the Flight Commander. When I walked into his office he said, "I hear you are having problems flying, I said not really and handed him my log book from the Fort Bragg Flying Club his expression and attitude changed. When he saw that I had previously soloed in 14 hours at the Flying Club, "In just 14 hours" he said and handed me the logbook back and said I'll be flying with you tomorrow; that he did. We flew rectangular patterns, slow flight, stalls and touch and gos. He then said pull over and let me out. I soloed that day and was assigned another Flight Instructor, Chief Warrant Officer Bob Lapan, who happened to also be white. He was a great instructor and an even better human being. He made flying fun. I had no more troubles flying the airplane. He taught me how to properly use the trim tabs and let the airplane fly itself with minor adjustments from me, he taught me to keep the nose on the horizon and on the numbers on the runway when landing and to maintain a steady rate of descent so as to remain above stall speed. I couldn't believe I touched the numbers just about every time.

My next set back came in the classroom when I was totally unprepared for the Meteorology block of instruction. When I came up a little short on Meteorology, my classmates and friends then Captains J.W. Hendrix and Dean Anderson stepped up to the plate and made sure my punishment was no more than being set back for two weeks. That would be the last time in my life that I would have subject matter problems even if it meant studying until I dropped which I have managed to do a couple of times since then. As bad as I hated getting Set Back I simply thought back to my high school graduation motto," No Gains Without Pains" and painful that was, but all things happen for a reason. I was able to assist a couple of other students with meteorology and with navigation in the next group. They showed me as much appreciation as I felt for J.W. and Dean.

A day before we left Fort Stewart for Fort Rucker, J.W., who had left two weeks earlier, called med and told me a T42 had gone down with Steve and Jones on board along with their Instructor. I thought back to the fact that Steve had bought a boat and a new Grand Prix while we were at Fort Stewart. A couple of us had tried to talk him out of doing so since we were all going to Nam; his reply was "I want to do this because we all are going to Vietnam. I want to enjoy this while I can." I'm so glad he bought the boat and the car. We all enjoyed his boat on J.W.'s father's lake on Saturdays as a way of dealing with the stress of Flight School.

As we approached Fort Rucker a couple of days later, I was so devastated that I started looking on both sides of the road for any signs of the kind of skid marks caused by a skidding (crashing) aircraft because they still hadn't located the crash. As it turned out, Jones' sister, a psychic from Texas, had called and told Fort Rucker Officials where her brother's plane was and that he was still alive. She said it was near a mountain; the only problem was there were no mountains in that area. The mountain she saw in her vision of the crash was an Indian Mound and when her brother Warrant Officer Candidate Jones was found, it was determined that he was the last one to die, he was alive when she said he was. It all seemed like a dram to us and it wasn't because death was new to us. Many of us were combat veterans. It was because this just wasn't supposed to happen to that instructor and our classmates, not in flight school.

The next thing we knew we were in one of the base chapels attending a Memorial Service for the three of them. From that day on there were empty spots in our hearts. At that point in my life I don't think I had seen a wife in so much pain because of the loss of her soldier. A few days later we learned that the crash had been caused by a Flat Spin entered into while practicing single engine stalls. And just think we all thought the multi-engine planes were safer, we didn't even wear flight helmets or parachutes in the T42 Beach Barons.

Fort Rucker Alabama was no Fort Stewart Georgia, it was much larger, there seemed to be thousands of flight students there, four times a day the sky was darkened by airplanes and helicopters, when the morning flyers flew out to the training areas and when they returned and when the afternoon flyers repeated those flights. Like Fort Stewart we were expected to relieve the tension by working hard and playing hard. Although the class members didn't seem quite as close as we were at Fort Stewart, Fridays were the exception. We all went to the Fort Rucker Officers Club for Happy Hour, a Happy Hour like no other on earth. There were so many Officers at Fort Rucker that the O Club gave away airplanes as bingo prizes, and actually had the plane sitting outside the Officers Club. One Friday as I stood at the bar waiting to be served my cherry coke, I noticed a Captain standing at the other end of the bar staring at me, we both checked each other's name tags and started walking towards each other. He was Captain Martin Jagles, my Company Commander from the 8th Infantry Division in Germany. The last time he had seen me I was an E-5. He paid me a great compliment by saying I was a great looking officer and that I looked like an Aviator in my flight suit.

On 11 December 1970 I took my cross-country check ride completing my multi-engine check out in T42 AC number 12912. The following week the fun began, as we started our Tactical training using an O-1 Bird Dog Tail Dragger. On 14 December, I found myself in the front seat of the tandem seating O-1 executing spins, slow flight and stalls. During steep approaches and landings I earned my second nickname/call sign from the Instructors. The first was Black Baron for obvious reasons, the second was Silky because of the way I was able to make near perfect descents and lands during all phases of the O-1 training, thanks to CWO Bob Lapan. We took our tactical check rides and graduated on 9 March 1971.

When I walked across the stage to receive my wings I wasn't alone. My father was there in spirit, as were Steve and Jones, Chief Warrant Officer Bob Lapan from Fort Stewart was sitting in the audience wearing a big grin. After graduation I went over and thanked him for being there, took him to lunch and headed back to Fort Bragg for two week leave to spend time with the family before reporting to Fort McClellan, Alabama where I would spend several months before reporting to Vietnam for my second tour of duty – my first as an Aviator.

Velma insisted on remaining in North Carolina until after Brian Fitzgerald was born. Alabama had earned such a bad reputation during the sixties, some wives simply didn't want Alabama on their children's birth certificates and Velma didn't think her little boy who would share President John F Kennedy's middle name should be born there either. Although we had come a long way since the days of Dr. Martin Luther King, Jr. and the Kennedy brothers, stand taken by our wives spoke volumes about things not yet accomplished, and the women in our corners.

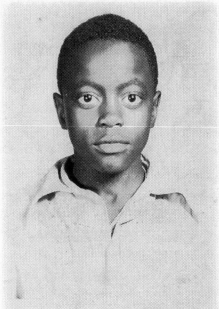

SCHOOL DAYS 1948-49

John Bailey in 1949, the year he wrote the poem Challenge,
which was registered with the Library of Congress
in 1983. Registration number 3-567-090.

Captain John H. Bailey II preparing to take off on a mission
from Phu Loi, South Vietnam during the Spring Offensive.

Robert and Jane Atkinson at the home of
the Bailey's in Missouri City, TX. LTC
Atkinson earned three Distinguished
Flying Crosses in Vietnam. Robert and
John were friends from early childhood.

Theathel Wells, childhood
friend of John formerly
of Drew, Mississippi who
now lives in Chicago.

Mr. and Mrs. Robert W.
Atkinson, proud parents of
LTC Robert W. Atkinson, Jr

Lieutenant Bailey performing Jump Master duties at
Ft. Campbell, Kentucky in October 1967.

PFC John H. Bailey II, 1960, Fort Bragg, NC

General Creighton Abrams, Jr. presenting First Lieutenant
Bailey the Arcom with "V" Device for leading an ambush
patrol in Vietnam that captured 112 detainees.

First Lieutenants Bailey and Thames at Camp Eagle,
South Vietnam. They are still great friends.

Velma Bailey with the catch of the day, 1970 at Ft. Stewart, GA.

Captain and Mrs. J.W. Hendrix, now General and Mrs. J.W. Hendrix.

John with God Mother, Mrs. Edna Wattley Hoxie, in Philadelphia 1973

US Marine and Vietnam Veteran Donald R. Isaac. Cousin to John who was lost in a helicopter crash in 1973 shortly after returning home from Nam.

Captain's John H. Bailey II and Art Nichols
at Phu Loi, South Vietnam, 1972.

Alcorn State Military Science Department Staff 1977. Left to right;
Front Row: Major Neasman, LTC Wright, and Captain Hill, Second
Row: SFC Garrett, Captain Washington, and Captain Bailey.

Major Generals Robinson and Mote assisting Mrs. Bailey at the Pinning Ceremony of Brigadier General Bailey in 1991, making him the first African American to attain the rank of General in the State Guard.

Ruth Bailey during a photo session in Missouri City, TX.

Brigadier General Bailey with Boy Scout Troop
103 in Nacogdoches, TX, Aug 1991.

The wedding of Captain John H. Bailey III to Renee.
Left to right: Renee's parents, Mr. & Mrs. James
Rayford, Renee, John, Velma, and Brian Bailey.

Dee Dee, Yolanda,
Will, and Terry at
Will's wedding

The wedding of Harriett to Celestine Muoneke.

Harriett's wedding.

Will and Cheryl celebrating their marriage.

John H. Bailey III, member of the McKinney High School's
State Championship Football Team in 1979.

Chris Bailey of McKinney High Basketball fame, who went on to follow in
his fathers footsteps by attending Embry-Riddle Aeronautical University.

Dee Dee; Baby Girl and the one we depend on.

Brian and Camesha Bailey.

Terry; who graduated
with honors in Biology
from Millsaps College in
Jackson, Mississippi as well
as being a 1982 inductee
into "Who's Who Among
Students In American
Universities and Colleges."

Yolanda; whose essence and spirit
is sorely missed. An exceptionally
loving and dedicated parent who
found the time to earn two degrees.

John H. Bailey II

Ruth with Uncle Deid of McKinney, Texas

Vernon and Izora Gales
of Jefferson County
Mississippi. Now residents
of Ft. Hood, TX.

Jack Bailey. Sigma Chi Always.

Amanda, Administrative Assistant of Bailey Military Institute
and former student at Clear Creek High School.

Cadets from Clear Creek HS at the CCISD Military Ball 1998-1999.

Raider Team, the pride of Clear Creek JROTC

Lieutenant Mel Starks, 101st Airborne Division
at Camp Eagle, South Vietnam, 1968

Cutting of the Corps cake at the 25th Annual Military Ball.

Generals Bailey and Thames with Ruth at Camp Mabry, Austin, Texas

Bronze Eagles Receiving 2011 Team Trophy Operation Skyhook

Champions of the 2011 Skyhook Competition in Pinebluff, Arkansas. 3rd, 4th, 5th, and 7th from the left are Treasurer Marvin Smith, Chairman of the Board Fred Lewis, President of the Bronze Eagles Anthony Hall, Vice President Ed Kimbrough. Major General Retired John Bailey II is 3rd from the right.

Officers from the Unified Veterans of America. From left to right; Garlon Arnic- Treasurer, Revlon Bell- President, Curley Hampton- Chaplin, Lori Victorian- Secretary, Ralph Wilson- Vice President. Not pictured is current President Willie Mitchell.

Brothers of the Ft. Bend County Alumni Chapter of Sigma Chi Fraternity. Officers pictured are Glenn Gill President, Jim Hayes Vice President, Jack Bailey Secretary, and Rudy Cuellar Treasurer.

Ruth's family gathering in Natchez Mississippi.
Among those pictured are Ruth's Siblings; Left to Right: James Harris, Cheryl Brinkley, Hayes Harris III, Cary Harris, David Harris, Lorna Anderson, Susan Harris, all seated around their mother, Mrs. Sarah Ruby Harris. Not pictured is her brother Keith Harris.

Bailey Military Institute's
Cadets at the Buffalo Soldiers
Museum in Houston, Texas.

Bailey Military
Institute's crest.

Bailey Military Institute's Board of Trustees. Officers
pictured are: Lori Carrigan-President, Roberto DeLeon-Vice
President and Ed Abram-Senior Military Instructor.

Chapter Seven

Fixed Wing Aviator

I reported into Fort McClellan on Friday and flew my first mission that Saturday. I was still unpacking when a phone call came into my quarters telling me to report to the airfield to fly co-pilot with Captain Roy Riddle, the unit's Operations Officer. I put on my flight suit, jumped into my Austin Healy Sprite and headed to the airfield not knowing where we were flying to or anything else. As I approached the flight line I noticed that the propeller on the U-6 Beaver was already turning. I grabbed my flight bag, my aviator sunglasses and double-timed to the plane. Roy could tell I was excited about getting there late so he started directing me away from the big propeller on that big radial engine. I jumped into the right seat and no sooner had I buckled in, Roy started taxiing to the hot spot pointing to the checklist, my job as Co-pilot, as I looked back I saw sky divers sitting on the floor of the plane giving me thumbs up, thus telling me my first mission would be dropping sky divers.

We flew away from the base and started making large climbing circles until we were at altitude, about that time I noticed that the ground crew had popped smoke and a couple of minutes later we were giving the first man out the "Go Ahead" sign. As soon as the last jumper cleared the plane we banked left and started a steep descent, being a former Paratrooper, I made sure the number of deployed parachutes matched the number of Jumpers that had exited our plane. With the Jumpers out, chutes open, nothing could go wrong – right? Wrong. As we began to return to Base, the only engine the Beaver had began to sputter. Captain Riddle and I looked at each other and said, "What was that?" then looked at the fuel gauge at the same time. He then looked at me and said "The crew who flew the plane last night didn't top it off!" I said, "Isn't that SOP?" Roy said, "Stop thinking about SOP and start thinking about this power off landing we are about to make!" The Prop turned freely although the engine sputtered until we landed. We refueled and took off with our second sortie. The lesson learned for me that day was to never again allow myself to be rushed where I couldn't make sure the person I was flying with had followed the entire checklist, or I had completed that task myself.

That Monday I met the rest of the Crew assigned to Fort McClellan's Aviation Division. Our Boss was Lieutenant Colonel Bagwell who had been recalled to active duty because of the war in Vietnam. Of the pilots assigned to Fort McClellan's Aviation Division, My favorites were CWO Corky Smith, CWO Herb Keaty, CWO Martin and Lieutenant Leon Butler also a newly assigned Aviator from Flight School. Our mission was to provide aviation support for the Base Commander, Brigadier General Mildred Bailey. We were a small staff with a small fleet of aircraft; our Fixed-Wing aircraft were one U-8, one U-6, one T-41, a couple of Huey's made up our Rotary Wing Fleet. Fort McClellan was home to the Women's Army Corps and the United States Army Chemical Corps, what and explosive combination of must have on your team of soldiers. Life on the Little Alabama base proved to be quite rewarding. In addition to the Flight Crew at the Airfield, I met the Public Affairs Officer who was also from Texas. His name was Major John Jones. Major Jones enjoyed Happy Hour and we would meet him at the Club each Friday and Saturday evening for several hours of good clean fun! As an unaccompanied Officer I lived in the Bachelors Officers Quarters. I went fishing when I wanted to and didn't have a set time to leave the O Club. In addition to the O Club, because most of us were just biding time at McClellan en route to Vietnam, the Old Man gave us one day of Rest & Relaxation each week and demanded that we field a respectable softball team in addition to remaining mission ready which we did.

Other than training missions most of what we did were pax hauls, equipment runs to For Benning, Georgia and maintenance flights to Fort Gordon Georgia. Lieutenant Butler and I were the only ones honored to fly blasting caps from Anniston Army Depot to various ports for overseas shipments in one of the C47 aircraft, this bird was more powerful than anything either of us had flown because it had two 2,000 horse power engines. Other than having to manually lower and raise the landing gear, flying the C47 was fun and a great experience and twice the size of anything else we had to fly at Fort McClellan, Alabama.

My next important mission was a cross-country night flight to haul Inspectors to Marion Alabama to inspect a United States Army Reserve Units Training Session. That night I reaffirmed my nighttime navigation abilities, each checkpoint fell within the wingspan of U-6 and the time checked out to the minute. I wish every Army Aviator could have flown the Beaver for with its huge slanted wings it seemed to be just floating there through the emerging molecules. The passengers even stated that it was one of the best flights they had been on.

In Mid-May several of us boarded a Huey Helicopter and headed to Birmingham Alabama for the Federal Aviation Administration Commercial Written Examination. We didn't need it to fly for the Army we just wanted it. About three weeks later I received my Commercial Pilot Airplane Single and Multi-Engine Land Instruments Certificate Number 2096460. A couple of weeks later I flew the first of two missions to Fort Bragg North Carolina, this was great because I was able to see the family and take the kids out to see the Airplane their Dad was flying. On the way there I dropped Lieutenant Butler off at a small airport near Elizabethtown, North Carolina. His whole family was there to see him. That left me and the Sergeant who had to attend a class at Ft Bragg to fly the rest of the way. One of the elderly gentlemen there to meet Lieutenant Butler said to me when you take off tip the wings for us; we have never seen a colored pilot before. After my maximum performance take off I rocked the wings several times for him. They were all waiting when I returned to pick LT Butler. How I wished all Americans could be that appreciative of us during our most unpopular war.

A funny thing happened to me while trying to be a Good Samaritan. One evening while in flight operations I received a call that said due to weather a flight from our unit had to remain over night at their destination. Lieutenant Butler's name was on the mission board. I wasn't able to contact his wife Eleanor so I decided to be the nice guy and stop by his house, ring the doorbell and tell Eleanor. As luck would have it my car just stopped about a mile from his house. I walked the rest of the way, hoping I could get Eleanor to give me a ride back to the BOQ where I was staying. When I rung the doorbell Leon came to the door. I simply said, "What are you doing here?" He said, "I live here. What are you doing here?" After explaining I was there to tell Eleanor he wouldn't be back tonight he gave me a ride back to my little yellow as a lemon sports car. And yes, it started right up, but stopped before I could get going. I simply said thank God. Leon told everyone and we laughed about it the rest of my stay at Fort McClellan.

One slow day in May as we hung out in the game room, Captain Roy Riddle stuck his head in the door and asked if anyone wanted to learn to fly the C-47. Leon Butler and I looked at each other and after pausing a second or two to give the others a fair chance we almost broke our necks getting our hands up. We were told to report to the Anniston Airport the next morning to meet the crew and be briefed. Our first flight was with a civilian Pilot named Rocket Man to a North Carolina port hauling blasting caps to be sent over seas. Our second flight was with a retired Air Force Officer named Jack Blume. He was an exceptional pilot and great instructor this time we flew to Kessler Air Force Base Mississippi hauling ammunition. I would fly with one or the other a couple of more times logging a total of 28.5 hours. Corky Smith and I would fly to Fort Benning Georgia a couple of times Corky was a perfectionist he earned his Civilian Flight Instructor rating that summer.

I call my next mission, the flight that almost didn't happen. I was assigned the mission of flying the Post Exchange Officer to Biloxi Mississippi. I met him at the Airport, when he arrived I had already conducted the pre-flight inspection. He walked over to the plane I introduced myself and he said, "Give me a minute." The next thing I knew Captain Riddle was there talking to him. Roy walked over to me and said he had some concerns. I assured him that you could handle the mission. The PX Officer had on civilian clothes so I assumed he was a civilian.

Between Fort McClellan and Biloxi there was absolutely no verbal communication between us. I refused to look his way or explain what I was doing to him. I just flew the airplane as fast as I could without red lining. A funny thing happened upon arrival; Approach Control vectored us out over the Gulf for quite a distance before turning us inbound. He was squirming in his seat, had he been a better passenger I would have explained "Glide Ratio" to him. He asked, "Do you know we only have one engine?" I looked at him and smiled. We arrived back at Fort McClellan around 18:30 hours after logging five hours and fifty minutes. I said "Good bye" and reported for Happy Hour. Roy had told several of the other pilots what had happened. I simply had no comments. The experience was bad enough.

Brian was born on the 31st of July, I moved the family to For McClellan in mid-August, by then I had received orders for Vietnam and thought it best to spend time with the family before shipping out.

We had cookouts block parties and did the usual things. Velma met and got to know Corky's wife Pat and their children but time flew by and it was time to move the family into our new house in McKinney. We began the long drawn out process of saying good-bye. One weekend we drove back to Fayetteville to say good-bye to our neighbors there.

After returning to Fort McClellan and getting our furniture ready for shipment, we took the kids on a last shopping spree to Anniston, the great little town near our base. I made a grave error and decided to leave our dog Snoopy outside while we were gone, when we returned he was nowhere to be found that literally broke our hearts.

Who would take our beloved four-legged family member? We posted signs, offered rewards, checked the pound and everywhere we could imagine but no Snoopy. On our way to McKinney, Texas we promised Harriett, John and Chris a new puppy, Brian Fitzgerald was still quite young and blowing bubbles, he could care less about a puppy. While in McKinney I visited coach Evans and all of my other favorite teachers, extended family and friends and then limited my time to my immediate family who were unable to hide their concerns about me returning to Vietnam for a second tour. About a week after departing McKinney I was flying my first combat mission with the 219th Aviation Company (Headhunters) out of Pleiku, South Vietnam. The 219th was organic to the 52nd Aviation Battalion, and was commanded by Major Edwin R. Clubb, I was assigned to the position of Second Platoon Commander. Not like traditional Army units, in aviation battalions the company commanders were Major's and the platoon commanders were Captains. It was in the 219th that I met Captain Art Nichols and Lieutenant Bernard Gunn. As it turned out Lieutenant Gunn was also a graduate of Tuskegee Institute and knew the late Captain Lee Grimsley, "Green Eyes", my other friend from Tuskegee Institute whom I had the honor of serving with during my first combat tour with the 101st Airborne Division. It just didn't seem right that Lee was no longer with us, according to LT Gunn; Green Eyes was also his nickname at Tuskegee. It sure would be nice to punch off a few 2.75 mm rockets at a VC unit in the area of operations where Lee was killed. I really wish the people back home marching in the streets protesting against our presence here and calling us baby killers could just once feel what those of us who have lost friends or relatives in this God forsaken place feels, as Lieutenant Grimsley and I had much dialogue concerning the need to support the men and women in harms way whether the war was popular or not, after all they are protecting the rights of those who are protesting.

The 219th Reconnaissance Airplane Company had an impressive combat record since arriving in Vietnam, when you approached company headquarters you were greeted by a statute of a masculine headhunter, knife in one hand, head in the other. A welcome sight and morale builder to warriors, an over kill to a couple of reporters from the media standing there discussing it as I walked into the orderly room. We flew more Route and area Reconnaissance missions than search and destroy missions while in the 219[t.h.]. Because we were going through the process of turning the war over to the Vietnamese my stay at Pleiku would end in a couple of months and many of us received orders to the 74th R.A.C at Phu Loi which was closer to the Cambodian border and much farther from Laos. Pleiku had been a great assignment, home away from home for Thanksgiving, Christmas and the New Year which all went well, but I had one more towering assignment before leaving for Phu Loi, that was to serve as Keystone Project Officer which require me to supervise the inventory and cataloging of thousands of pieces of equipment that included aircraft, repair parts, weapons, weapon systems, clothing and other unit property. I was then required to serve as Convoy Commander leading the massive convoy through the winding mountain roads between Pleiku and Qui Nhon to the Property Disposal facility. Because we were standing down we did not have the necessary resources for aerial convoy coverage, which caused me much concern, so I called on ancestral guardians from Africa to Texas, which meant all should go well for the young drivers and guards on the vehicles that trailed me. Upon returning to Pleiku, we stood down and had an awards ceremony that was mainly for those with less than 90 days left and would be going home other than being reassigned to another fixed wing aviation units in Vietnam. Major Clubb thanked me for leading the convoy, turning in the equipment, clearing the property book and for serving as second platoon commander, although for a short period of time. We then went our separate ways for our new assignments; some of us were assigned to the 11th Combat Aviation Battalion's 74th Reconnaissance Airplane Company, "Aloft". The airfield was about the same size as the one at Pleiku but seemed to have a larger helicopter presence on the other side of the runway. One of the best features at the new base was the Black Virgin Mountain that was clearly visible after taking off from Phu Loi as well as from the border between South Vietnam and Cambodia where we often flew in support of the Special Forces Camp in close proximity to the base of the huge mountain that depended on us for much support, and we enjoyed providing it. Sometimes we just flew over their small camp to check on them. I had two jobs in the 74th, a fixed wing aviator and Service Platoon commander, which involved me in aircraft maintenance, thanks to a crew of hard working NCO's aircraft mechanics, and crew chiefs, the second job was relatively easy. I took good care of the troops, managed production control, and participated in as many test flights as I could. The level of readiness of our fleet of aircraft was never less than 97%. The first job, Fixed Wing Aviator was somewhat more demanding. The 74th was assigned to Military Region II, with the mission of flying visual and route reconnaissance missions in eastern South Vietnam, providing many valuable photographs of suspected enemy encampments and resupply routes for G2, Third Regional Assistance Command and G2 18th ARVN Division

On 9 January 1972, I flew an area reconnaissance mission just north of the Cambodian border, what I saw excited me. There were several signs that signaled POW Camps, although that far south, they were probably temporary campsites until the POW'S could be moved to North Vietnam, we took valuable photographs of garden plots near streams, no people were spotted within 25 miles in either directions of the site, and stones were arranged so as to give initials and dates. We assumed the initials were of POW's and the dates were the dates they were captured we took photos of the area, fly over after flyover. After our final pass we called in our first shot at report for that mission, thankfully our bird wasn't hit, our crew chiefs didn't like bullet holes in airplanes, neither did their Service Platoon Commander. The thankless part of our job was that we would never know if those letters in stone we photographed matched any of our many missing airmen and soldiers, we certainly hoped they would.

While flying to Saigon from Cu Chi on 9 June 1972 chatter on air to air indicated that John Paul Vann had gone down in his helicopter. His death was quite a loss to our efforts in Vietnam and a shame because we were standing down and he probably would have been going home soon.

On 29 July I put the war behind me and flew home for Brian's first birthday on 31 July 1972. I was home for eight days and spent all of my time with family except a couple of hours visiting with Coach and Mrs. Evans.

Thanks to being able to log C47 time at Fort McClelland I was able to log 21 right seat combat missions in Vietnam, the language barrier was not a problem. There seems to be an international language in the cockpit. South Vietnamese also attended flight school at Fort Rucker and made great pilots.

While at Long Binh I would occasionally see LT Bernard

Gunn, I met another officer there that would remain a great friend, Captain Leonard Leassear. After leaving for Saigon I would only see Bernard Gunn once again and that was at the 1972 Homecoming of Tuskegee. Fortunately I now get to see Leonard Leassear every other month at our Men for Change meeting in Houston. Bernard now lives in Birmingham, Alabama. Neither LT Gunn nor I have since heard from Captain Art Nichols, who now lives in California.

Being assigned to Saigon should have been great but it was quite dangerous there. In the seventies throwing acid in the face of Americans became popular, as did spreading razor sharp thin wires across the road to cut soldiers driving or riding in Jeeps with the windshields down. It was now October and my time in Saigon was soon over and after the flight home assignment to the Advance Course was next on the agenda for me. While in the advance course at Aberdeen I would log my flight time in OH 58 Helicopters though I was not Rotary Wing rated. While there I was able to visit with my God Mother while she visited her niece and her husband, Mr. and Mrs. Sam Cook, in Philadelphia. My cousin, Donald R. Isaac, from St. Louis just home from Vietnam was lost in a Marine helicopter crash at the Naval Air Station in Memphis. He joined the Marine Aviation Branch because I was in Aviation. Now he was gone, leaving a young wife and two small sons, not to mention his mother, my first cousin, Betty Isaac. After graduating from the Advanced Course and departing Aberdeen, I would only be able to see that wonderful place again at annual Ordnance Corps Balls, but APG still holds a special place in my heart.

CHAPTER EIGHT

Brotherhood of Men

UPON GRADUATING FROM THE ADVANCED Course in November 1973, I was assigned to Embry-Riddle Aeronautical University, Daytona Beach, Florida to complete the final sixty hours toward my Bachelors Degree in Aeronautical Studies. We shipped our furniture, loaded the kids in my Volkswagen and Velma's new Cutlass Supreme and headed to Florida, our first trip to the Sunshine State. Velma reminded me that we should fill up the tanks before crossing Georgia so we wouldn't have to depend on anyone in Alabama selling us gas. All went well. We reached Florida without a hitch, found a nice four-bedroom apartment on the Halifax River I reported to Embry-Riddle and Velma enrolled at Bethune-Cookman College. As an active duty military student I had to report to Dean J.H. Spears who was our counselor and monitored our progress. He told me that as a Captain with four years time in grade I would be one of the Senior Officers on campus and that I should plan to be one of the social magnets for the Vets. With that information we joined a local church for spiritual leadership example and hosted a cocktail party about every 90 days to get the group together. After a couple parties the other officers kicked in and began hosting social gatherings.

Embry-Riddle was a small campus located on the Daytona Beach Airport Grounds. Having missed out on the normal college life of a nineteen year old I took Dean Spears advice about leadership and involvement to heart. I became Sports Editor for the University Newspaper, the Avion, served as Chief Justice for the Student Court, which I was well prepared for thanks to the law training and mock trials offered during Officer Candidate School, I assisted the Student Government association with blood drives, worked as a volunteer during student registration and assisted with graduation exercises.

I also served as a member of the Army Aviation Association, and worked on off campus activities with the Volusia County Detention Auxiliary Board for Youth, served as guest speaker for Mainland High School's Career Day and appeared on local television for discussion of Embry-Riddle, Army Aviation and Campus Organizations. I personally coordinated the establishment of an Army ROTC cross enrollment program between Stetson University and Bethune Cookman College. I would have done more, but I couldn't put anything else in my schedule.

In addition to president Jack Hunt and Dean J.H. Spears, Mrs. M. H. McLemore was a favorite educator of mine. Maybe the fact that she taught all of the upper level speech communication and English Literature classes, my favorites, had something to do with it.

There were less than 3,500 students on campus, even very few females and African Americans. Because of it's Veteran population which included many active duty officers and Warrant Officers you saw students driving some top of the line automobiles like Jaguars and Corvettes. Embry was different in other ways as well. We didn't have football or track or homecoming parades. We didn't even have our own gym or field house. But what we did have we were proud of and supported to the hilt. We had soccer, baseball, basketball, fencing, and a competing flight team. Our claim to fame was that we played baseball against Harvard and occasionally beat them. Academically we were into Science Technology Engineering and Math. Some of our students were actually building aircraft on the Embry-Riddle Campus. Embry-Riddle remains the top Aeronautical University in the country.

My academic briefing forever changed how I talked to soldiers planning to participate in under graduate degree completion courses, we were told to get the easy electives out of the way and take the more difficult courses once we became full time students. The truth be known you only transfer your semester hours not that great GPA you earned at the local community college completing the easy electives, therefore the Chemistry, Physics, and Trig you waited to take would be waiting for you.

The other area of college life that stood tall at Embry-Riddle was its team of college fraternities. To name a few Sigma Chi, Lambda Chi, and Delta Chi headed the list. In that no traditional black fraternity was on campus we met at my apartment and formed a social club called Brothers of the Wind, and no, you didn't have to be black to join. Another viable organization on campus was it's Veterans Club, quite different from most other organizations, there we had students who had flown in combat, several of whom had been seriously wounded, and those who had spent time as prisoners of war. In spite of the hardships they had faced, during my two years tenure at ERAU we only lost two. One that was flying a tourist helicopter that had a rotor blade strike with a large bird and crash into shallow waters along Daytona's beach front, and a suicide caused by an abrupt divorce within a year and a half after returning home from Nam. Several of us Vets literally camped out near the crash site until a huge CH34 owned by the Doan Company hoisted the small copter out the water about 36 hours later. Those two incidents caused the Vets club to become a closer-knit group. We counseled each other and helped each other with the more difficult courses and hosted on campus happy hours on Saturdays.

I was quite active in the Veterans Club until one day as I walked across campus and a couple of students were handing out flyers for their fraternity recruitment drives. I received flyers from Sigma Chi and Delta Chi. After attending the rally hosted by Sigma Chi and hearing Hugh Mills talk about the fraternity and it's Constantine Chapter formed during the Civil War I didn't need to look any further. I was hooked. Finding out that my favorite cowboy, John Wayne, would be my fraternity brother didn't hurt either. Sigma Chi was quite active on campus. The fraternity owned a frat house on Ridgewood Avenue. It was an old motel with a huge swimming pool out back and a great mascot named Fred J. Ford, quite a Sig to say he had four legs. I was not the traditional pledge; I was thirty-two years old, black, and married with four kids. These differences I couldn't help, but I made darn sure no other differences existed with me. I participated in all the chapter activities (Eta Iota) and worked very hard as a pledge. My wife thought I had lost my mind for being the one to integrate a white fraternity in the South. But I didn't see it as integrating a fraternity; I saw it as joining one. I played on the intramural football team, dressed up as Captain America and rode a tricycle, and last but not least, landed on campus in a helicopter dressed as Blacula and bit a fellow Sigma Chi on the neck to kick off a campus blood drive. You tell me that didn't help you forget two tours of duty in Vietnam.

One of my best Sigma Chi experiences was to realize

just how great my brothers were when someone suggested I be dropped because I was in my thirties and married. Hugh Mills, Jeff Kennedy, and Morris Ford stood up for me. Yes, Morris Ford was Fred Ford's namesake. And most of my pledge class said if I wasn't good enough neither were they. I found my white cross and became a Sigma Chi in 1974. My next great Sigma Chi experience was my little brother John Valentino, what a great young man. He never noticed a difference in our skin color and neither did I, and neither should anyone else, ever. About 15 years ago when I attended the 25th anniversary I saw John and met his family. It was quite a reunion. John was a successful Airline Pilot and I imagine he is still flying since he is about 15 years younger than I am. John and I still exchange Christmas cards.

One of my strangest Sigma Chi experiences came one evening when I was working in the front yard of the Frat House as it started to rain as I started inside the house. When I looked back and noticed a short person standing at the bus stop. I ran over and invited him to come in out of the rain. He did, but missed his bus to Orlando. Since our frat house was previously a motel we had extra rooms and I talked the brothers into giving him one for the night. The next day I received a call saying "Jack get your butt over here now." I expected the worse. When I arrived several of the brothers were there with devilish smiles on their faces. They said "Look in that brief case and tell us what you see." As I looked in the case I noticed what appeared to be a small white dress. I picked it up and would you know it was a little KKK robe that the little person had left there when he went out to catch his bus the next morning. Everyone got a big laugh at the expression on my face. Someone suggested I find him and give it back since I was such a nice guy. I showed absolutely no interest. A funny thing happens to me each time I'm at a baseball game and I see the three Ks used to signify three strikes, I think about our experience with the little person.

In 1995 I was chosen to serve on the Board of Trustees for Embry-Riddle Aeronautical University, quite an honor for me. I was at the time a commander in the Military Forces of Texas and heading the Military Science Department of Clear Creek Independent School District and couldn't imagine serving more than one tour on the board. During that time we managed to get an Embry-Riddle Campus in the Houston area that is still growing today. In 1996 I was honored when my fraternity bestowed the honor of Significant Sig on me, which brought me much joy. Over the years I have been careful to make sure I never did one thing to cause the brotherhood to regret granting membership to me, or want to deny membership to anyone else because of me. I still support National and have been a member of the Eta Iota's 1855 Club for 16 years as of 2012. I am also a charter member of the Fort Bend County Alumni Chapter of Sigma Chi and the Houston Alumni Chapter and was able to meet Sigma Chi Brother Bud Adams, owner of the Tennessee Titans, formerly the Houston Oilers. And more recently Houston Texan Quarterback T.J. Yates, his father, and grandfather, all members of Sigma Chi.

It seems that I have been able to run across Sigma Chis at most places I've been since becoming one. Upon my arrival in Mississippi I was in a bank opening an account and met a Sigma Chi by the name of Hyde Jenkins. When I became a member of the General's Staff at Camp Mabry, Texas I met a Sigma Chi Brother Karl McLeod of the University of Houston, Karl would become my Chief of Staff after I earned my Second Star and became Commanding General. While on the Board of Trustees for Embry-Riddle University I made several trips back to the Daytona Beach Campus, visited the old frat house and talked to the brothers there. I also saw several members of my pledge class and my little brother John Valentino, Bob Butterworth, and Morris Ford to name a few at the 25th anniversary of the Eta Iota Chapter. I still talk to Jeff Kennedy from time to time.

As far as Brothers of the Wind is concerned I searched for members each visit, but found no one. Surprisingly I saw an article about the club in one of the Embry-Riddle publications. I will once again attempt to locate them on my next visit.

Because Houston, Texas is so far from Daytona Beach I seldom see any Sigma Chis from Eta Iota, therefore it was a pleasant surprise to learn that brother Hough Mills would be the guest speaker at the 2009 Wild Game Dinner sponsored by the Houston Alumni Chapter. Hugh gave a great speech and is still the great guy I remember him to be at Embry-Riddle. Hugh was also an exceptional combat aviator. Only a few Army Aviators can match his record in Vietnam.

At Alcorn State University, my next assignment after Embry-Riddle, I would be the only Sigma Chi on campus but when I attended the Alpha Phi Alpha fraternity annual ball I made sure ΣΧ was on the wall with the Greek letters of the other fraternities in attendance. I was told that a couple of years after I left there they were still putting Sigma Chi on the wall, they have invited me back on several occasions.

One of my strongest, most satisfying memories of my tenure at Embry-Riddle was the time I was able to spend with four great little kids my father would have just loved and spoiled rotten, Harriett, John, Christopher, and Brian Bailey. I managed to do all the great things with them I could only dream of doing with my father. We went camping once per month, we went fishing once a week, I taught John and Chris to be expert marksmen as the US Army had taught me, and we went Disney World in Orlando. The most fun came when on Thanksgiving we got together and played our neighbors football. Although two tours in Vietnam where I had experienced tense situations had led me to the Catholic Church, we joined a Baptist Church for the sake of being together. Baptist was about as far as Velma wanted to drift from her family church home, the Methodist Church.

CHAPTER NINE

Mississippi My Way

My degree from Embry-Riddle Aeronautical University meant more to me than words could express, not only did it mean that a member of my immediate family had graduated from college, but since a college degree was one of the variables that determined social class, my having earned one was an ego booster and moved us up a notch. Shortly after meeting the requirements for my degree I took some quiet time and thanked God for clearing the path that led me to the US Army where with his help I had remained safe through two combat tours and academically qualifying for the officer under graduate completion course. The next great thing the Army was about to do for me was to send me back to the place where my condition was so grave that for a while I lived with my grandmother in a one-room house with no running water. Now I was going back to that place. I would not only serve as the University's Aviation Officer and an Assistant Professor of Military Science but could also earn a Masters Degree paid for by the GI Bill and experience an upper middle class environment in a place where I didn't know one existed for my people when I was a child.

I arrived at Alcorn State University about 14:00 hours on 14 July 1975, would have arrived there much earlier had the person I sought directions from in Natchez, Mississippi not told me to take the scenic route that bordered the banks of the Mississippi River and it would take me straight to the Alcorn Campus in Lorman. When I arrived at the Campus Chapel that housed the Military Science Department I met Ms Carrie Ross the head secretary for the department. She directed me to the Professor of Military Science, Lieutenant Colonel Ed Wright, a graduate of Southern University, Baton Rouge, Louisiana. His first words to me were "I was just about to call and report you AWOL. I expected you about ten this morning." I hoped that was a joke, but didn't ask. Later that day I met Captain Lloyd Napoleon Hill, a great Army officer who would become another of my life long friends. Everyone else assigned to the department were attending ROTC Summer Camp at Fort Riley, Kansas. Colonel Wright introduced me to the president, Dr. Walter Washington and Dr. Norris Edney; Dr. Washington stated that I was there because he personally requested that the Aviation officer be an African American, just as he expected the Professor of Military Science and Command Sergeant Major to be. He explained his feelings to me by saying the University of Mississippi didn't have a Black PMS, Sergeant, Major, or Aviation Officer. I had no problems with his reasoning; in fact I was in total agreement.

As I toured the campus meeting other staff and faculty members I realized Alcorn State's wealth of intellectuals, not simply in name, but in reality. I also learned that the staff and faculty probably represented the best Mississippi and the great country I had represented in combat on two occasions had to offer and that they were committed to changing the lives of the approximately twenty-five hundred students on that campus. I rented a four-bedroom apartment in Fayette, Mississippi, a small town just south of the Alcorn campus. I had searched for a place in Port Gibson because of its Civil

War history but couldn't find the size place I needed for a wife and four budding kids. In Fayette I was introduced to the town mayor, Charles Evers, brother of the late Civil Rights leader Medgar Evers. Mr. Evers welcomed me with open arms and invited me to serve on several committees.

I thought all was well until about three weeks into our stay in Mississippi, home of my birth. I went home from work and found the two women in my life in tears. I asked Harriett what was wrong and she said, "Mom's crying." I asked her "Is that the reason you're crying?" She said, "Yes." I closed the door for privacy and asked Velma what was wrong and she said, "I don't want to be here and my mother doesn't want me here." So my next comment was "But I'm here. It's my duty station for the next three years." That was when she explained that when we were kids her mother's nephew had been stationed in Mississippi and had been murdered here and she wanted to return to McKinney and live in our home there until my tour at Alcorn was over. I spent the next few days trying to change her mind, but to no avail.

We came up with a plan. She would go home, enroll the kids in McKinney public schools, go to work as a nurse with her mother at Wysong Hospital and I would find a smaller place to live and continue my duties at ASU. Her deal also required me to fly or drive home once per month.

At Alcorn my additional duties were property officer and cross enrollment instructor at Utica Junior College near Jackson, Mississippi. I also became the advisor to the perishing rifles who gave me an abbreviated initiation so I would appreciate what they had to go through to become members. The PR's were one of the campuses proudest fraternities and their drill team drew much applause at the many parades they participated in at Alcorn and surrounding townships.

Early on in my tenure at Alcorn State University I found time to visit the Mississippi Delta, the little town of Drew looked about the same as it did a lifetime ago, in 1954. When I visited I was able to find most of the people I needed to say hello to. My first visit was with the Wells family, Mr. Sammy Wells seemed a little older but Mrs. Ethel looked the same. I met some of their children for the first time. My friends Sammy Jr. and Theathel had followed the path of many of Drew's blacks and moved up north for work and in some cases better treatment. They had chosen Chicago. I next visited the Atkinsons and checked on Robert, he was still flying in the Air Force and his little brother Boyd had become an attorney. When I visited the Sheridan family I received the shock of my life. Mr. Sheridan, who had written me a letter while I was serving my first tour in Viet Nam, asked me why I decided to get an education. I told him my father had told me an education was black peoples key to a better life.

As I stood there in front of him with my chest covered with Pilot Wings, Senior Parachutist Wings, the Soldiers Medal for Heroism, Bronze Star with Oak Leaf Cluster, and Air Medals with Oak Leaf Clusters to name a few, I hoped he would comment on at least one. He never did, but he did ask me about Mrs. Betty, my grandmother who had lived in the one room house on his property and served as his cook and maid. He seemed saddened when I told him she had died in St. Louis in 1959. His wife, Mrs. Ruth Sheridan, looked about the same. She took time to look at every award I was wearing. Her eyes said she was proud of me. I proceeded to the flats, it had changed very little, and a couple of the old clubs had closed, as had the old movie house, which was my favorite. I went by the school where I had spent so many fun filled days in first and second grade. From there I drove to the Looney place but no one was home and the Miller place to see if I could find any of the Staples. On my way back to Alcorn I drove by the area where my father had taken me in search of my mother's grave. I couldn't remember what happened between there and Beulah, where my father and stepmother were buried. Since 90% of the people in that area where share croppers I didn't see a soul I remembered, each time I would call a name I was told they had either died or moved up north.

Upon returning to Alcorn I met with the Colonel who told me we needed more cadets in ROTC because Prairie View had about 1,000 Cadets. I started working on plans to present to Major Neasman, the second in command, when he returned from Summer Camp. Colonel Wright wanted us to set up a table during registration while at the same time attempt to recruit them into the Army ROTC program. All went well and our enrollment doubled that year and grew each subsequent year through 1979. After planning for recruiting we began planning for the upcoming football and basketball seasons. The Color Guard would present colors at each home game and all ROTC staff members would be in attendance.

In helping direct us in the right professional direction we were encouraged to meet as many members of the staff and faculty as we could and to sell Army ROTC to them, which seemed to work quite well. Among the personnel I was able to meet early on were Mr. Marino Casem, Athletic Director and Head Football Coach, Dr. Grant Dungee the Track Coach, Dean James Bolden, Dean of Student Affairs, Mr. Dave Whitney the well known Basketball Coach, Dr. Melvin Williams, Dean of Academic Affairs, Wiley Jones, Senior Accountant, Dr. Virginia Caples, Chairperson, Department of Home Economics, P. L. Fluker of the Agriculture Department,

John Wall, and Al Johnson. As time passed I would meet the rest of the staff and faculty. Although I had attended several colleges and universities enroute to my Bachelors Degree this was my first experience with a historically black institution except for attending sports events at Bethune-Cookman with Velma while at Embry-Riddle. To say the least, I was highly impressed with the level of professionalism I found at Little Alcorn State. It was only little in size. 90% of the students at Alcorn State were Mississippians, 99% were black, like me. That spoke volumes about the opportunities education made possible for people who needed it the most.

I was quite pleased to learn that the wonders of Alcorn State were being repeated at four other historically black colleges and universities in my home state, where the staff and faculty were equally committed to changing the lives of students who attended their institutions, no matter the color of their skin. Alcorn State had its share of Caucasian and foreign instructors who were equally devoted to the art of teaching. An understanding of how much teaching and learning meant to these professional caused me to concentrate less on the learning levels ROTE and understanding and spend more time on the application and correlation levels. Even today I have an occasional student drop by and tell me how much he or she enjoyed and remembered from my classes at Alcorn State. In retrospect I think I learned as much about Mississippi and it's black middle class as they learned about Oral Communication, Military History, Tactics and the Art of Leadership and Aviation from my lectures, practical exercises and demonstrations.

The next major event on the agenda was the first football game of the season against one of the first historically black colleges I had ever heard of, Grambling State University. The game was to be played at the New Orleans Super Dome. The trip from Alcorn State to New Orleans was like a never-ending convoy of Mississippi license plates. We filled several hotels and motels where we would return to after the game to visit the several hospitality suites hosted by various department heads. It reminded you of a good old-fashioned military happy hour multiplied by 12. The football game was a different story, Grambling didn't know they were supposed to cooperate and allow our gathering of fun and fan fare to continue. They beat us 27 to 3, but our team showed plenty of potential. We had players like All American Lawrence Pillars, Cecil Martin, Augusta Lee and Roynell Young, who played for the Philadelphia Eagles in Super Bowl XV and the 1988 Pro Bowl known as the Fog Bowl. He would later found The Pro-Vision Academy of Houston, Texas, where I was honored to teach Flight Technology. Pillars would go on to an exceptional career with the San Francisco 49ers, bringing much pride to the Reservation. Alcorn State ended the season with an overall record of 6-5-1 defeating such major competition as Delaware State, North Carolina Central, Texas Southern, and Jackson State. Coach Marino Casem and Mrs. Casem were all round leaders on the Alcorn Campus, from an Academic Athletic and social standpoint, hosting after game social gatherings, following home games, and hospitality suites for away games.

As I gained more exposure to the townships surrounding the Alcorn State campus I was able to get to know the people and their culture. One of my first moves was to find me a church home. The town of Fayette, Mississippi offered the closest place of worship for Catholics, Saint Ann Catholic Church. It was a small structure with a basement. The priest was Father Morrissey who had been involved in the local community since the struggle for civil rights in the sixties. Saint Ann was the only integrated church in the little town of Fayette. The only thing I found odd about it was during Mass the whites sat on one side of the aisle and the blacks sat on the other. As I sat there one Sunday I couldn't help but wonder which side would God be pleased with if he showed up for Mass, the side who wanted to be separate or the side who could care less where others sat. I couldn't wait to ask Father what that was about, he said there weren't enough Catholics in the town to justify two churches so that seating arrangement was adopted. He agreed with me that it was time to change that, but we never did. The Brinkley family, two of whom I was honored to teach, Margaret and Shirley was perhaps the biggest family at Saint Ann. Sadly I had to attend the funeral of one of their family members who died in a motorcycle accident. Father Morrissey was proud of the fact that his Parrish was integrated, I often joked that he held the wine chalice to his face too long during communion, his answer was he had to make sure it was good enough for the rest of us. Once when he decided to go into the basement to see if the wine had been delivered he tripped and fell over the case of wine that had been left there by the deliveryman. When he told me why he was wearing a cast I laughed and he hastily told me I needed to attend confession.

Perhaps the most intriguing person I met in Fayette was it's Mayor Charles Evers, brother to the late Civil Rights leader Medgar Evers. Mayor Evers was a real politician, he stayed busy running for office or supporting someone who was running for office. One of the single biggest activities in the state of Mississippi was the annual Mississippi Homecoming Celebration hosted by the citizens of Fayette each spring. It drew celebrities from around the country, it was there that I met the famous guitarist BB King, Archie Bell, and Mohammed Ali. I also got a chance to see an old Army acquaintance of mine from my days with the 8th Infantry Division in Germany, Captain Kris Kristofferson. We caught up on old times. He told me that mutual acquaintances of ours, Chief Warrant Officer Randall and CWO Hoot Gibson had both served in Viet Nam and made it home safely. Captain Kristofferson was a helicopter pilot in Germany and spent much time singing for us at the Rod and Gun Club. He was pleased to learn that I had become an officer and most importantly the Army Aviator I had dreamed of becoming. BB King and Kristofferson put on quite a show together in Fayette, Mississippi.

Through my association with the Mayor I was able to fly BB King from Jackson to Natchez, which was quite a flight. We talked about his guitar Lucille, sang a few of his favorites and I gave him the controls for a few minutes after learning he had taken flight lessons. He flew quite well. Because of the strict rules concerning entertainers flying in small aircraft, instead of flying direct cross country from Jackson to Natchez I parallel interstate 20 from Jackson to Vicksburg and stayed between highway 61 and the Mississippi River from Vicksburg to Natchez. I felt my chances of negotiating a highway or water landing was better than a tree landing. It was also in the little town of Fayette that I met Mrs. Rosalyn Carter who personally asked me to vote for her husband for President of the United States, and yes, I did.

Because I lived in Fayette, most of my stay in Mississippi I was able to observe the culture of the people of Jefferson and it's surrounding counties more than that of the rest of the area. To say the least, 60% of the people of those counties blew the stereotypes I had come to know over the years out of the water.

Their knowledge patterns enabled them to discuss the Fine Arts and Humanities to great lengths and you could observe them passing that knowledge on to their kids and grandkids. I almost caused an accident while driving near the Natchez Trace one day and passed a house with its front yard filled with sculptures by Lavern Hamberlin you didn't have to stare at to identify. And then there were the literature and music legends whose roots led back to Mississippi. Eudora Welty of Death of a Traveling Salesman fame, Richard Wright from nearby Natchez who's works included Black Boy and Native Son, William Faulkner, author of As I Lay Dying, Opera Singer Leontyne Price and her brother Brigadier General George Price, Tennessee Williams, writer of A Street Car Named Desire, Playwright James Earl Jones, Musicians BB King and Elvis Pressley and an up and coming television show co-anchor by the name of Oprah Winfrey, who would go on to become the standard bearer for television talk shows and the list goes on. I quickly concluded that the only thing Mississippi needed was industry, professional sports, and fewer people obsessed with the color of ones skin.

As far as my tenure at Alcorn State goes I must revisit ROTC Summer Camp at Fort Riley, Kansas. By the time I would participate in my first camp, most instructors in the department were on their second and third trip. The leadership shown by our PMS, Lt Colonel Wright was exceptional; the idea was to make sure that each of our Cadets successfully completed the course. Although each of us instructors were assigned to different training companies, the plan called for us to meet at the end of each day to find out if we could be of assistance to the Alcorn Cadets and to give them pep talks, it worked out just fine for all concerned. We felt good about the abilities of our Cadets, they had confidence in themselves and the ROTC Region Headquarters didn't have to worry about recycling any of our Cadets or dropping them from the program.

Each trip to Fort Riley gave me a chance to service on the Tactics Committee, which I found quite intriguing since I was basically an Infantryman wearing the "shell of flames" insignia of the Ordinance Corps. That Committee was quite a challenge and offered the Cadets an opportunity to prepare an issue operations order before moving out and reacting to every imaginable challenge a unit moving from point A to point B in a combat environment could expect to face. The tactical problem was where everything else the cadets had been taught came together in one training scenario.

In that, Fort Riley, Kansas was just four miles from Junction City, home of Kansas State University, spirits were high and there were several places that catered to the instructors there for Summer Camp. We decided to make Kennedy's Claim our hangout, because it was a private establishment with atmosphere of an officers club.

Because of the nature of our assignments at Fort Riley we didn't car pool, each of us drove our individual vehicles. I think Captain Lemarse Washington (Killer) and I had the most fun. He in his Corvette, sunglasses, driving gloves, and pipe and me in my MGB, attire likewise, of course he could leave me in the dust whenever he wanted to. The only negative thing about being at Fort Riley was being away from the Airplane and not being able to take off and land on Alcorn's wonderful little grass strip.

Other than football, Alcorn was known for it's great basketball therefore I must mention Coach and Mrs. Dave Whitney who took the basketball community in and around Jefferson and Clayborne Counties to a new level. The level of enthusiasm and professionalism demonstrated by the coaches, players and their support groups rubbed off on all basketball lovers within a hundred miles of Alcorn State, little kids wanted Alcorn State Jerseys, and the high school hoopers tried to play like them. Coach Whitney and Coach Walker led their teams to SWAC championship with such ease that we thought they were invincible. The game to top all games was when little Alcorn State defeated Mississippi State in the first round of the play offs when Larry Smith hit a shot at the buzzer to win the game. In my opinion it was that game that opened the doors for small historically black colleges to be placed on the schedule of the larger historically white colleges. Larry Smith would go on to play pro ball with the Houston Rockets. Alcorn's assistant basketball coach Lonnie Walker and his wife Shirley offered much to Alcorn's second most popular sport as well. Mrs. Walker coached the Alcorn State University's women's basketball team who terrorized the Southwester Athletic Conference women's league.

Alcorn sports drew more loyal fan support than most large city historically black institutions. Most games were standing room only. The closest thing I've witnessed to Alcorn was Tuskegee University, which is in a league of it's own in more ways than one.

Like any other assignment in the military with the duties you welcomed came those you would rather not be a part of. I was called on to be survival assistance officer on three occasions; two of those were in the city of Natchez. The first was a young specialist who lost his life in Germany the day before he was to depart there for home. I had known his uncle for a couple of years and met his mother and siblings while notifying them and preparing for his arrival from Germany, that particular duty took me back to 1967-68, 1971-72. I spoke with Specialist Rowan's mother several times since the funeral. She was still crying about the loss of her son. His uncle was a long time friend of Ruth's family.

The second was a young Army Reserve Major who was a member of one of Natchez's prominent families. He was lost while piloting an airplane near Fort Huachuca, Arizona. My job was to officially notify his wife on behalf of a grateful nation, upon my arrival important businessmen and bankers were already there. The wife waited until I completed my official remarks, hugged and thanked me for coming. That was my first time in one of Natchez's huge antebellum homes. My survival assistance duties were limited to the official notification and attending the graveside services. I called to check on Major Boggesse's family several times since then and spoke with Mrs. Boggesse once and her mother a couple of times. All was well.

As my tenure at Alcorn State continued to grow I decided to explore the rest that ASU had to offer, that was when I discovered the protective attitude of our leader, Dr. Walter Washington, he was all about protecting Alcorn's honors and doing whatever it took to stay in the Board of Regents good graces. Once when the staff and faculty received a pay raise he warned us not to go out and buy Mercedes for fear of appearing too affluent to the board. He didn't say anything about sport cars so I traded my old MG for a new white MGB with a black rag top and red and black racing stripes, back then most Army Aviators drove sports cars, today it seems that they drive pick up trucks. I tried to join them, but flipped my Ford Ranger a couple of times on the Lake Charles Bridge.

Because Mississippi was a great farming state one of the most important departments on campus was the Agriculture

Department, it prepared it's graduates to return home and properly manage the states farm land, much of it owned by African American families. In fact black families were losing so much land that some of the agriculture departments graduates were hired to monitor the sale of black owned farms. Among the fine instructors in that department were Mr. P.L. Fluker the president of the Alcorn State Flying Club and a great friend and Mr. E.N. Elliott. Mr. Fluker did whatever it took to keep the little grass strip operational and the airplane flying. Of Alcorn's small staff and faculty there were twenty-seven non-black staff and faculty members. The school of nursing had several non-black students.

As an institution of higher learning, Alcorn state has quite a history for it's Alumni to be proud of. Founded in 1871 it is the oldest public historically black land-grant institution in the United States and second oldest in the state of Mississippi. Alcorn started with eight faculty members. Today it has around 800 faculty and staff members and students from 30 states and 18 foreign countries and of it's 18 presidents, Dr. Washington had to have been one of it's most compassionate.

As far as the Military Science Department goes my mid tour staff members included LTC Wright, Major Hill, Major Neasman, Captain Washington, SFC Thomas, SFC Garrett, and myself. The civilian staff included Ms Carrie Ross and Ms Lillie Williams. Other instructors who joined us later that year and during following semesters included Major Tom Erby, MSG Doug Tillery, SGM Ben Troutman, Captain Andrea Morrison, SGM King, Major Luther Berry, LTC Norman Calhoun, SFC Massey, not a single one less committed than the one before him, the epitome of dedication and professionalism. In addition to LTC Dennis Hudson and

MAJ Paul Brown, several other cadets went on to achieve field grade rank. To mention a few, COL Betty Washington, COL Dwain Hill, LTC Larry McMillan, LTC Bobby Rayborn, MAJ James Rayborn, LTC Gwen Thames, MAJ Robert Baker, and MAJ Marshel Wilson.

LTC Norman Calhoun followed LTC Ed "Sie" Wright as the professor of Military Science at Alcorn State. One Friday I received a call at my Fayette, Mississippi office telling me that the LTC from the Army National Guard unit called saying my son who was a cadet in his unit had refused to cut the grass around the Armory and didn't want to perform and had implied that he refused to help, therefore he would be calling a meeting to recommend that John not receive his commission upon completing two years of college as the plan then authorized. It just so happened that I knew several soldiers in that unit who knew Cadet Bailey, when I asked them to give an honest evaluation of his performance as a Cadet and a soldier they informed me that he was as good as any other Cadet in the unit. They also informed me that the grass around the Armory was taken care of by civilian contractors, I found that very interesting. I arrived for the meeting early and asked him what was going on between Cadet Bailey and his unit. He stated that the Cadet had smarted off to one of the NCO's when told to go out and help cut the grass and he personally thought 19 year olds were too young for commissioning. What he didn't know was I had served with 19 year olds who were officers during my tours of duty in Viet Nam. Some came home with Silver Stars, Bronze Stars, and Purple Hearts. Somehow he missed the fact that the Major he had bad mouthed Cadet Bailey to earlier that morning was wearing a name tag that said BAILEY. He made his statement and I made mine. John was commissioned according to plans. I was tapped to help the local high school in Fayette get approved for an Army JROTC program, was offered and took the job as the Senior Army Instructor where I would remain until John completed college two years later. Unfortunately LTC Calhoun was killed in a vehicle accident the next year and Major Luther Berry, another exceptional officer, became acting Professor of Military Science until Colonel Clyde Blakely came on board. Luther and I remain friends to this day. He currently serves as the Director of Army Instruction for Fort Worth ISD. Upon arriving in the Houston area one of the young officers I met happened to be COL Berry's brother, who would also go on to attain the rank of Colonel.

Chapter Ten

"I Touch The Future; I Teach"

Jefferson County ISD

I DID NOT COIN THE phrase "I Touch The Future; I Teach," but in my mind there is no better way to express what educators do. Upon leaving federal service I had two choices, fly for South Central Air Transport (SCAT) at reduced salary or put my training in Education Administration and Supervision to work in a field that guaranteed me the satisfaction of working with young people, wearing the uniform I loved, and enjoying the camaraderie I had become accustomed to. I accepted the position of Senior Army Instructor for the Jefferson County Independent School District. Jefferson County is located in Southwest Mississippi.

The City of Fayette, the County seat, and only city in the county, was home to the School District, which included a high school, a junior high school, upper elementary school, and an elementary school. The schools were attended by students from the townships of Church Hill, Harrison, Lorman, Perth, Red Lick, Rodney, and Union Church. The County had a population of just 9,500 residents. Jefferson County had the highest percentage of Americans of African decent in the country and the county had little or no industry.

The School District was under the leadership of Dr. Marion Hayes. Mr. Daniel Smith was the Principal of Jefferson

County High School. Both were supporters of the ROTC program because of their relationship with Alcorn State and welcomed the Army's Junior Reserve Officer Training Corps, into the District.

Dr. Hayes authorized funds for a new building to house the program. Mr. Smith ensured that the JROTC staff and students were equal to all other departments on campus. My very first year I had an opening enrollment of one hundred and forty-eight cadets and had no assistant. About halfway through the second semester a young looking Sergeant First Class walked into my office and said, "Major Bailey, I understand you need a little help." My reply was "Yes, welcome aboard!" Although our enrollment always qualified us for a second Non-Commissioned Officer, to keep the district from having to share the salary of a third instructor, SFC Reo Maynard and I would spend the next three and a half years enjoying the best students Jefferson County and perhaps Mississippi had to offer, and doing whatever it took to succeed.

Because of Jefferson County's limited budget and small number of students between grades nine and twelve, Jefferson High didn't have money for the extra curricular activities some larger schools had, but it's football, basketball, and band were as popular as they were on larger campuses in metro areas. The students and band support all local activities. The new JROTC Color Guard and Drill Team became favorites for local parades in the neighboring Natchez, Alcorn State, and Jackson Mississippi.

Activities popular to our Cadets were the Annual Mississippi Homecoming, the Alcorn State Homecoming activities, and the Natchez Mardi Gras Parade. The Mississippi Homecoming event was sponsored by the City of Fayette under the leadership of Mayor Charles Evers, brother of slain

Civil Rights leader Medgar Evers. Mr. Evers had the power and character to pull the best for his homecoming weekend in addition to the money, famous people such as Jesse Jackson, Mohammed Ali, Robert Earl Jones, and an occasional football or basketball star. After becoming Mayor, Mr. Evers changed the face of Fayette's landscape. A clinic was build and named for his brother, an apartment complex was built in honor of the late Dr. Martin Luther King, Jr. and he sponsored a parade and celebration for local native astronaut Richard Truly upon completion of his first flight into space which was lead by the JROTC Color Guard and Drill Team. Also important to the Cadets and their parents was the JROTC Summer Camp held at Fort Rucker Alabama. We took thirty-two cadets as a new program attending it's first camp. Although the yellow bus ride left much to be desired, not one Cadet complained and they enthusiastically participated in each activity requesting to repeat the Leadership Reaction Course and Rappelling Tower.

As they completed high school the Cadets of Jefferson County also found raising their right hand and taking the Oath of Enlistment or Commission. Popular of the approximately 350 Cadets I was in contact with during my four-year stay in Jefferson County more than 65 raised their right hand and among that number, fourteen earned commissions through the Alcorn, Southern, and Jackson State ROTC programs and twenty-one became Non-Commissioned Officers. Desert Storm attracted the service of many, Iraqi Freedom demanded the service of even more, and several served multiple tours. I was fortunate to be present at Fort Hood for the send off of Sergeant First Class Vernon Gales on his second combat tour, I was also able to mentally revisit the toll combat tours have on spouses of those gone off to war, as I observed his wife

Izora, also a graduate of Jefferson County High and former Cadet, and like a daughter to me.

Two exceptional former Jefferson High Cadets were lost in automobile accidents, LT Lee Author Durrell, a graduate of Alcorn State and Sidney Harding a student and cadet at Southern University, both so full of life and promise. Those enrolled during the first four years of JROTC who excelled in military training and service were LT Lee Durrell, LT Lisa Smith, MAJ Inger Robinson, MAJ Trent Hudson, LTC Robert Kent, LTC Patrick Kent, COL Stephen Kent, LTC Vincent Thompson, SFC Vernon Gales, and SFC Ammie Griffin.

Some former cadets who would go on to excel in other than military careers were Cassandra Williams, who became a pharmacist, Lisa Williams who is a nurse, Kimmie Ware, Yolanda Robinson, Joan Walters, Patricia Oliver, Lamatha Jackson, Shirley Brown, and Brenda Turner who is a city manager in Fayette, MS, and Vincent Turner who now serves as principal of the Junior High School in Jefferson County and I'm sure there are those I am unaware of because that number continues to grow because of the heavy laden education culture in and around Alcorn State, which I wish all communities had. That culture seemed to make attending college the rule and not the exception. I only wish I could personally thank all the hard working staff and faculty members of the Jefferson County School District who believed in themselves and understood the importance of education and proceeded to turn little piles of sand into pyramids of diamonds. I love you all for what you did for our future.

At the halfway point of my tenure with the Jefferson County Independent School District the fact that I'm only human came to bear, Velma and I divorced. The survival mode

I became accustomed to as a small child in the Mississippi Delta and during my tours in Vietnam kicked in, and once again happiness was simply being alive and for me life needed to go on because I had much unfinished business.

In addition to serving as Senior Army Instructor, my remaining time in Jefferson County would find me serving as track coach and a defensive back coach for the Jefferson County High School football team. I have very fond memories of the latter. Before the game between Fayette and Natchez High, the Natchez Coach made a mistake and referred to the game with Jefferson County as a "gimme". I have rarely seen a group of kids practice with such heart and purpose. I thought back to my days with Coach Evans and Coach Jackson in McKinney and managed to get Coach Dunbar to go along with two plays we used during our district championship days. One was called Poison Ivy; the other was simply the quick kick. We came close to winning that game, but couldn't pull it off. South Natchez won the game, but by no means was it a "gimmie". The next week the phone rang off the hooks asking how we scored so many points against South Natchez High School. Our answer was simply; our kids played up to their potential. They always knew they were appreciated by the many ways we rewarded them after each game. One thing we added at Jefferson High School was to purchase helmet ornaments and present them for tackles, sacks, key blocks, passes caught, and touchdowns. Morale was sky high.

Clear Creek ISD

In November 1983 Ruth and I were married and moved into a ranch house on 25 acres west of Fayette near the Natchez Trace. She continued to serve as an AT&T Group Manager in Natchez, a job she was great at. In August 1984 we moved to Houston, TX, where Ruth was to be hired as a Group Manager. Unfortunately the person she was replacing changed her mind. After being told by the Director of Army Instruction of Houston ISD's JROTC program that he didn't need anymore black Senior Army Instructors and to try Clear Creek ISD. I did just that. I can't count the times I have thanked him for that advice. By the way, he too was black. I also decided to continue my military career by joining the Texas Military Forces, which consists of the Army National Guard, Air National Guard, and the State Guard. Clear Creek ISD was headquartered in League City and served northeast Galveston County; it was 23 miles southeast of Houston. There were approximately 35,000 people living in the city limits of League City. The middle class rated in the top 11% of the state of Texas. Other town's supported by Clear Creek ISD were Webster, Seabrook, Clear Lake Shores, Clear Lake, and part of Friendswood.

Clear Creek ISD was under the leadership of Dr. John F. Ward, the Superintendent of Schools, who set the standard for district leadership involvement in the JROTC program, his level of support would be followed by Dr. John Wilson and Dr. Sandra Mossman. Clear Creek High School, where I would be billeted, was headed by Mr. Ralph Parr, a truly exceptional leader with outstanding people skills. When I arrived the staff, faculty, and student body at Clear Creek High were still reeling from the recent loss of Major Kenneth Forren, the founding Senior Army Instructor of Clear Creek High JROTC, whom I had no intentions of trying to replace. The Non-Commissioned Officer on staff was a very capable Sergeant First Class by the name of Harvey Jerdon who had pretty much ran the program by himself the previous school year due to the Major's illness. Other than getting the opening enrollment report together for Region, our most important objective according to him was to prepare for the first booster club meeting, which he declared would be like no other ever held in the district. He was right, there was standing room only when Ruth and I walked in, SFC Jerdon introduced us to the Booster Club President, Mrs. Hreha, who introduced me to the parents and few students present. In my opening remarks I assured them that I was not there to replace Major Forren, but was there to take what he had started to the next level, by whatever means necessary and that with their help I felt quite sure we would accomplish that mission. Some of the parents I met that night were the Blankenships, the Sweeneys, the Hreahs, the Harts and the Villerreals, Cadet Jason Moore, Albert Hreha, Kenneth Sweeny, and Billy Hart were among the Cadets present.

Of the instructors I was able to meet early on were coach Buddy Carlisle, one of the basketball coaches, I would learn later that the field house at Clear Creek was named after his father, Coach George B. Carlisle, secretaries Nancy LeBlanc and Paula Radicioni, Ms. Gwen Cash the only other African American instructor on campus, when I first saw Gwen I thought she was a student, she still looks the same, Mr. Jerry Johnson, Dr. John Peterson, Ms. Mary Ann McBride, Mr. Richard Kremer, Mr. Kim Benning, Mr. Tommy Bishop, Mr. and Mrs. Michael Hudson, my baseball buddies, who went out of their way to welcome me and make me feel at home.

There were two high schools in Clear Creek ISD. I was initially required to teach two classes on each campus. Because it was home to the Johnson Space Center with it's support base most of the families there were upper middle class or higher. In 1984 CCISD had one JROTC parent unit, Clear Creek High School and one cross enrollment unit Clear

Lake High School. Mr. Ed Taylor, a former Army officer who was most supportive of high school and college ROTC programs, headed Clear Lake. Whatever the program needed Ed provided, including a regulation rappelling tower making us one of the few schools in the Houston area to have one. The tower really came in handy when preparing our cadets for JROTC Summer Camp. After getting the enrollment up and stable I applied for Clear Lake High to have it's own JROTC program, which was quickly approved because of the overall academic standing of Clear Lake High. I initially assigned SGM Leonard Valeen, a retired Airborne Ranger, Vietnam Veteran, and recipient of the Soldier's Medal to the SAI position. I gave him the authority to recruit an assistant; his choice was Master Sergeant Bob Heaton, a Green Beret. They made a great team.

My assistant at the Creek campus was then MSG Harold Laranang who was also a Green Beret and holder of the Silver Star from Viet Nam. Not long after that we had a third high school in the district, Clear Brook High in Friendswood. In addition to managing the program I spent my instructional duties between Clear Creek and Clear Brook until one day a former student of mine at Alcorn State knocked on my door looking for a job. I introduced him to Dr. Sandra Mossman, the principal of Clear Brook, who would later go on to become Superintendent of Schools, he was hired to head the cross enrollment program there and remained the Senior Army Instructor of that program until Clear Lake High School needed his presence to lead the JROTC program there because the Army wanted Officers as Senior Army Instructors. Paul remained the SAI of Clear Lake High until Clear Springs High opened in 2007, he was assisted at Lake by SFC Michael Turnage. At that time he also assumed the duties of JROTC coordinator for CCISD. Since my retirement a fifth High School, Clear Falls, has been added and has a National Defense Cadet Corps program.

In 1996 I was successful in getting my plan to place a similar program at the Intermediate School level approved by the district. I called it the Leadership Development Corps. I wrote a curriculum for Leadership and Leadership Lab and adopted the curriculum approved by the Military Order of World Wars for the academic portion of the curriculum. That program quickly grew to seven schools in CCISD, two in HISD, and my friend LTC Luther Berry would go on to implement the curriculum in Fort Worth ISD.

As with the resources in other management fields, the JROTC instructor's most important resource was also its people, to be more specific, the Cadets around which all else evolved. Clear Creek Independent School District was unusually blessed with talented and gifted students; thankfully the JROTC and LDC programs had their fair share. Today former Cadets are proudly among the ranks of Doctors, Attorneys, Engineers, Educators, and members of the Armed Forces. Of the activities enjoyed by the CCISD Corps of Cadets Ranger Swim Team, Raider Team, Rifle Team, Saber Guard and Orienteering Team were tops. Those activities that were a part of intra district competitions; CCISD schools were the usual winners. I must also add that absolutely nothing topped the staff briefings given by the Battalion Staffs during the Annual Formal Inspections and the Joint Annual Military Ball usually attended by the 98% of the cadets from all three campuses. Counting the cadets, their guests, instructors, and a few parents, attendance would usually reach 500 and was held at the luxurious South Shore

Harbour Resort and Conference Center until we out grew it.

The CCISD Military Science Department would eventually end up with a staff of fourteen instructors and a football field full of Cadets proudly carrying their Colors, flashing their Sabers and standing tall for our Annual Reviews, quite fitting for a stadium to be named in honor of fallen heroes from all branches of the service. Adding to the pride I felt each day was the fact that three members of the staff were former students of mine. LTC Dennis Hudson and Major Earnest Paul Brown both commissioned through the Senior ROTC program at Alcorn State University, and Major Kevin Reams, an Eagle Scout, who graduated from Clear Creek High School and was a State Guard Commissionee. The rest of the department staff was made up of professionals from various branches of the Armed Forces, with the high school division all being retired Army, and the intermediate school division being made up of Army, Marine Corps, Coast Guard, and State Guard. Together they made a great combined team when it came to getting our Cadets ready for Summer Camp, Senior ROTC, the US Military Academy or a branch of the Armed Forces, or Reserve Components.

To our advantage the city of Houston boasted a wealth of activities for JROTC units. Houston's Bluebonnet Military Skills meet was Granddaddy of them all, with Galveston Ball, Willow Ridge, LaPorte and Channel View hosting smaller meets. Clear Creek ISD hosts the Challenger Seven Memorial Military Skills meet for Intermediate School LDC programs. The high school meets usually consisted of Academic Team, Color Guard, Drill Team, Physical Fitness Team, Orienteering, Ranger Swim Team and Rifle Team. Lieutenant Colonel Willie Bratcher, the HISD Director of

Army Instruction ran the best meet in the area and hosted the annual JROTC Summer Camp held at Camp Bullis, TX for the Houston area schools.

Over the years Clear Creek Schools boasted several exceptional Cadets from across the district, and whereas it would be impossible to name them all, it is imperative that I name a few who excelled in the Corps of Cadets and then went on to do well in their chosen professions, military or civilian.

Listed in order of campus seniority are several Cadets from each high school campus. From Clear Creek High hailed Jason Moore the former Battalion Commander who held 95% of the Army JROTC Ribbons and earned a scholarship to Texas A&M, Brad Hayes and Kelly Blankenship who earned scholarships to prairie View A&M University where Brad would go on to become the field goal kicker and earn the title of "White Shadow" on the Football Team. During prairie Views rebuilding period his Field Goals were often the only points scored, I was so proud of those two for deciding to attend an historically black College as non blacks, I have always believed that integration was a two way street. Also from Creek were Major Angel Brito who's father MSG Brito still serves and the Army Instructor at Clear Brook High School, Captain Billy O'Briant, Sergeants Aaron and Jacob Klopp, SFC Robert Burd, Lieutenant Donald Flannery, Captain Mike Whitten, and Major Kyle Hathaway, Lieutenant Melissa Pringle, Lieutenant Aaron Gordon who is now attending US Army Flight School, Torren Davis who served in Desert Storm, and Michael Kissal who is currently serving in Afghanistan, just a few of the Commissioned Officers produced by the Clear Creek Battalion, either through OCS, Senior ROTC, or one of the Academies. One such Cadet is Air Force Academy

Cadet Luke Duncavish who began his Cadet training in our sixth grade LDC program, remaining a Cadet until graduating from high school and earning a slot at the US Air Force Academy. And last but not least, those who excelled in other than military careers like Doctor Eric Serrano, Attorneys Ericka Hutchinson and Billy Hart, Educators Gail Smith, and Joe Blankenship, Businesswoman Mishelene Bell-Baker, Nurse Eunice Rivera (Barbara Ann), Officer Kevin Greer, Officer Brian Goldstein, Eric Mayberry, Lorraine Everett, Leah Sanford who decided to marry a Bailey, Cara Rugg who I gave away at her wedding, Michael LeBlanc who went on to New Mexico Military Institute, former Battalion Commander Mary Brown now a student at University of Texas, her sister Michelle, a recent graduate of Stanford University's Doctoral program, Ryan Roy a Texas business man and Amanda Roberts who is the Administrative Assistant of Bailey Military Institute, a 501(c)3 Private Leadership School founded by the Bailey family.

Although Lake High did not officially become a separate unit until about twenty years after Clear Creek, it was no slacker in terms of exceptional alumni. Among them were Chief Warrant Officer Damon Sanger who flew Apaches during Dessert Shield Dessert Storm, Texas A&M graduate Captain Jada Ching (Green Eyes III), who gave me that nauseated feeling of having one of my own daughters in harms way while she served in Iraq. She was thoughtful enough to invite Paul Brown, her SAI at Clear Lake High and me to a special commissioning celebration after graduation where she posed with us for photographs that she placed in special Texas A&M frames before presenting them to us. That selfless act spoke volumes to the two of us. Devin Buffington went on to earn a commission in the Louisiana National Guard. There were also several Academy and Military School graduates, among them Major Paul Licate, Norwich University, Captain Ellen Gelzleman, Air Force Academy and now a C17 pilot, Lieutenant Commander Marcus Seeger, Navy, and Adam Gittleman, a West Point Graduate. Excelling in the Non Commissioned Officer ranks were US Paratroopers Ken Tucker and Ken Sweeney. Sergeant Tucker who married Kelly Blankenship went on to make a career out of the US Army and still serving on active duty. Another Lake Alumni is Adam Wickerson who is in his 4th year at the Naval Academy, keeping the Wickerson family tradition alive. Unfortunately one member of the Clear Lake JROTC Battalion was lost in Iraq, Sergeant Eric Duckworth. Clear Lake High School also boasts having a member of the Martin family in the Corps for the past 15 years. Mary G., the last, will graduate in 2014.

The third JROTC program to come on board was Clear Brook High School located in Friendswood, another upper middle class to affluent or opulent community who's other high school did not have nor did the administrators want a JROTC program. The school only had students who had formed a military club with posters, model planes and vehicles to show for it. After a couple of visits with the principal I stopped going. I've never learned to beg anybody for anything. I instructed the kids to ask their parents to enroll them in Clear Brook High School.

Like Clear Creek and Clear Lake High Schools, Clear Brook would become an exceptional program in a short period of time because it had established it's credibility as a cross enrollment program and we had subjected them to the same grueling standards required by the Brigade Annual Formal Inspection Team from the power point briefing given by the Battalion Staff to the mock formal inspections using the exact check list, used by the Brigade inspectors. Dr. Sandra Mossman participated in our programs and sang our praises. She probably would have become Commander of Cadet Command had she chosen the military as a career.

Another exceptional leader of the Clear Brook family was Dr. Carol Wilson, she simply carried a big stick and she didn't speak softly either. Dr. Wilson gave one of the best speeches at our combined Military Ball that I have ever heard. Us military types often joked about the fact that most men couldn't look at Dr. Wilson just once, but since she was married to an undertaker most men played it safe.

Each campus was blessed with great assistant principals. Mr. Steve Kees, a Marine Corps Veteran was no exception. He too was quite supportive of our program and assisted us in many ways. Some of the cadets who excelled in JROTC at Clear Brook were Cadet Abercrumby, who went on to West Point and Cadet Sunshine Basset, whom I shall never forget. Sunshine was a Native American. Having grown up in North Texas not far from the Oklahoma border I met many first Americans as a kid and enjoyed the experience; therefore Sunshine was one of my favorite Cadets. After returning from Christmas holidays I was asking the cadets what they had received for Christmas, Sunshine looked at me as only she could and said "A tomahawk". I gave the class a couple of minutes to stop laughing and went on with my class. Although I asked a few more questions, paused and then called on a cadet to answer, the name Sunshine simply couldn't come out of my mouth. Just one of the many wonderful memories I have of my Clear Brook classes.

About fourteen months prior to my retirement from Clear Creek ISD I received an e-mail apprising me of the fact that a fourth high school would be built in the vicinity of Creekside

Intermediate School. They asked me to meet a representative of the contracting company to discuss the needs of the JROTC program. At that time my District Director's office wasn't located on a High School campus, but my SAI office was still at Clear Creek. Knowing that I was recommending Major Brown to be my replacement I included him in the process and we came up with a model of what future JROTC areas should look like in CCISD. All went well except the size of the rifle range, which would need to be increased in size when the next school was built. When the new school, Clear Spring was completed another great educator and friend Gail Love became it's principal.

Also playing important roles in the success of the JROTC program in CCISD were the assistant principals such as Mr. George McKinnis of Clear Creek, Mr. Bob Ingram at Clear Lake, and Mr. Steve Kees at Clear Brook. The two exceptional NCOs assisting me at Creek during my final years were SFC Marc Sepulveda and SFC Doug Lein. Of equal importance were the counselors and booster clubs on each campus. The assistant principals were the arbitrators between the principals and the Senior Army Instructors. The booster clubs held monthly meetings and raised funds to purchase all items not provided by the US Army. The District pitched in and provided transportation for all trips except Summer Camp and the trip to the annual Texas A&M University football game.

The Leadership Development Corps was fully funded by Clear Creek ISD, including the salary for one full time instructor on an eleven-month contract to allow for teaching at the Leadership Camp conducted in June or July. Since my retirement Clear Creek ISD has built a fifth high school that now has a National Defense Cadet Corps (NDCC) unit. I'm also proud to say that the Pearland and Onalaska programs are both still going strong. Pearland has a JROTC program and Onalaska has a local Civil Cadets Corps unit. Teaching broadened my horizons and added new luster to my life.

Bailey Military Institute and St. Francis of Assisi

Thinking I would spend my time fishing, flying, playing golf and enjoying my six grand kids, I retired from CCISD in 2007, ten years after retiring from the Texas Military Forces. I now spend my time as a volunteer administrator and instructor at Bailey Military Institute and it's cross enrollment program at Saint Francis of Assisi Catholic School in Houston, TX., in addition to serving as an Adjunct Professor in the Aviation Science Department at Texas Southern University. Bailey Military Institute offers Leadership training for students attending schools that do not offer Leadership Development, NDCC, or JROTC. BMI is accredited by the National Association of Private Schools and is a member of the Texas Association of Non Public Schools. It is also a 501(c)3 non-profit cooperation. Long range plans for BMI are to purchase property and build a campus in Fort Bend County that will include dormitories and establish the school as a Military Junior College with classes beginning at 6th grade. In an effort to reach the maximum number of students BMI cross-enrolled St. Francis of Assisi Catholic School, located in Houston's 5th Ward.

The Bailey family founded and named the school in honor of the small measures of success I was able to achieve against insurmountable odds which in their minds would say to future generations; If John made his dreams come true, so can you.

CHAPTER ELEVEN

The Military Forces of Texas

BECOMING AN ARMY JROTC INSTRUCTOR offered those of us who took that challenge to heart, an opportunity to keep performing similar tasks to what we had spent much of our lives doing, however something was still missing for many of us, the camaraderie that was afforded by the culture of the total military community that simply can not be found elsewhere and the challenges offered by the ever complexing pyramid of authority that soldiers learn to live by.

For those reasons, I decided to apply for a commission under title 32 section 109 to go along with my commission under title 10. USC. Title 32 of the United States code covers State Military Forces, the National Guard, Air National Guard and State Guard for all 50 states, though only 35 states have active State Guards, all are able to activate them. Their mission is to supplement the National Guard and to assume their mission once they are activated. In 1985 I was commissioned in the State Guard with my federal rank of Major. I was sworn in by Lieutenant Colonel John Echoff, the Commander of the 202nd Military Police Battalion and assigned to the position S-3, Operations and Training Officer. Colonel Echoff instructed me to make sure each monthly drill was found to be challenging by the troops. My reply was simply "Not a problem". Because of my time in grade and proven track record in the short time I had been in the Guard, I was promoted to Lieutenant Colonel on 29 September 1986 and transferred to Headquarters Second MP Group and assigned to the position of Group Executive Officer under the Leadership of the hard charging Colonel Joe Bailey who strongly believed in self discipline, unquestioned loyalty mission accomplishment, and leadership by example, some times challenging in federal forces not to mention the all volunteer state forces. I spent much of my time serving as an arbitrator between the five Battalion Commanders and the Group Commander. Our greatest challenge that your was preparing for and providing back up security in the vicinity of the San Jacinto Monument for President Regan's participation in the Sesquicentennial Celebration of Texas Independence.

Thanks to my exposure to Colonels with the last names of Beckton, Cushman, and Emmerson, all who would go on and become General Officers, I had a fairly decent leadership style of my own, which came in handy when I was told by Colonel Joe Bailey to go down to the intersection and tell the KKK they had less than thirty minutes to vacate the area. Captain Bob Dickson who was standing near by said "Sir, I'll take you in my Jeep," When we reached the intersection I exited the vehicle and asked who was in charge. A hooded, medium built man stepped forward and said "I am. How can I help you?" I said "The President of the United States is enroute and I am in charge of back up security and traffic control and wanted them to clear the area as soon as possible." He informed me that he and his people had a right to see the President. My reply was since I didn't know who was under those sheets and this is my assigned area of operations I expect them to be gone by the time I return. To my surprise, when I returned from reporting to the Commanding Officer, the area had been cleared.

On 14 May 1988 I was promoted to Colonel and assumed command of the Second Military Police Group. In keeping with the Command Philosophy of Major General Jim Robinson the Commanding General, my focus was on Mission Accomplishment, Training, Safety, Morale and Unit Funds. Our area of operations extended from Brenham to the Louisiana State line with Armories in Houston, Galveston, Texas City Baytown, Beaumont, Sugarland, Orange, Anahuac, and Port Arthur. One of my personal objectives was to improve the number of African Americans, Hispanic and females in the ranks of the State Guard. In so doing I was required to activate a sixth Battalion, it would be located in Anahuac for strategic reasons.

I appointed Colonel John Echoff to the position of Executive Officer; he did a great job for the guard and me. During my tenure I added Search and Rescue to the Second Group Mission. We would train at Camp Bullis Texas with maximum participation because we were doing something the young guardsmen and woman enjoyed I also added providing traffic and crowd control for the annual air show held at Ellington Field. Halfway through my tenure Lieutenant Colonel Bernard Belvin became the group Executive Officer.

In January 1991 I was promoted to Brigadier General and was appointed to the position of Deputy Commander of Operations and Training at Camp Mabry in Austin Texas.

I would find that not only had I been nominated by the sitting Commanding General but also by the two most recent commanders who knew I would have an uphill battle but wanted me to be given the opportunity to succeed. The first function Ruth and I had to participate in was the Grand Promotion Ceremony held in Houston. I am still grateful for all the efforts of military and civilians alike who made that a special moment for my family and me, I received congratulations from coast to coast thanks to Bob Dickson who in addition to being an outstanding guardsman, was an exceptional news correspondent. Instead of the one trip per month I had made to Camp Mabry as Commander of the Second Group, it now seemed as if I lived there.

My job as Deputy Commander for Operations and Training was more difficult than it should have been, mainly because I was up against a few Commanders who were of the "Good Ole Boy Network" who believed monthly drill was for whatever they wanted it to be for; we had no reason to interfere. Well having spent my active Army career in Airborne and Aviation assignments I simply did not understand "do nothing" and had no respect for the "Good Ole Boy Network." Thanks to the CG, Maj Gen Marlin Mote, I was able to initiate some changes in training. Physical training was added to all training schedules not just a few. The objectives and standards in the Military Police handbook became the doctrine by which training schedules and lesson plans were written and we increased the number of command inspections and visits. On occasions my Aid de Camp First Lieutenant Willie B. Williams also a licensed Pilot and I would fly to training sites, such as Beaumont, Anahuac, and Fort Walters, Texas. Lieutenant Williams' wife, Dee and Ruth would become close friends over the years and remain friends to this day. Thanks to their son Devin, I enjoyed many great Football and Baseball games of his Clear Lake High School teams. Devin was an exceptional all around athlete.

In an attempt to give the High School JROTC Cadet Teams an annual trip to Austin as many other sports teams already had, the Operations and Training Shop and I established a State Military Skills Meet to be held in Austin Texas. The event paid for itself because Color Guards, Drill Teams, Ranger Swim Teams, and Academics Teams who had placed first or second in a regional competition paid a registration fee to participate. The program remained quite popular for many years and was then moved to Texas A&M University under the leadership of BG Donald Johnson, a fellow Army Aviator and Vietnam Vet. Mrs. Johnson mastered the art of decoration for the Christmas holidays.

I remained in that position until 11 February 1994 when my Superior Officer and Commanding General, Major General Marlin Mote, retired, on that day I was promoted to Major General and appointed Commander of the State Guard. This assignment would make the obstacles I faced, as the first African American Colonel and Brigadier General seem like Sunday school. Many people in the State Military still had some difficult truths to face, and my promotion and assumption of the command gave them the platform they needed for an all out assault. It was then that I noticed a slight change in the way Ruth felt about participating in many of the Guard's social functions, but the important ones she held her own. To her an attack on me was an attack on the entire family. I was so proud of the stand she took on my behalf.

The first attack on me was to say that my alma mater Embry-Riddle Aeronautical University was not an accredited institution; therefore my degree was no good. Embry-Riddle's answer to that was to appoint me to the Board of Trustees. They next attacked my character by saying there was no way I could be a Sigma Chi because there were no black Sigma Chi's back in 1974. Colonel Karl McLeod, my Chief of Staff and himself a Sigma chi, set that record straight. Then the Grand Chapter appointed me a "Significant Sig." While 50%

of the full-time staff members were trying to find something wrong with me and block progress. I went about the business of planning and initiating a much needed paradigm shift. One of my first actions was to activate a Headquarters Company fully staffed at Camp Mabry to enhance the administrative posture of the personal, special and coordinating staffs. Next I initiated the rank of Warrant Officer for the State Guard, because I knew this would add stability to Administrative and Technical departments because Warrants did not have to leave their assignments for command time, they stayed in their career fields and got better with time. Ironically on the day we were to induct the first two Warrant Officers, one male and one female, I was approached by Major Reaghard, a member of the full-time staff, and informed that the appointments could not take place because G1 did not get the orders cut in time. I answered by saying, give me a sheet of paper, on it I wrote the words, "Verbal Orders of the Commanding General" the following personnel are appointed to the rank of Warrant Officer. They were CW2 Lloyd Sanchez, a former Command Sergeants Major and W01 Kimberly Mosier, a former Personnel Sergeant. After that incident the madness slowed down for a while and we were able to make a few necessary changes for the good of the Order. Among the next few changes we made were reorganizing a Judge Advocate General's Detachment to meet the ever increasing requirements associated with Mobilizing the National Guard for War and calling the State Guard to State active duty to assume the duties for the National Guard. Organizing the Texas State Guard Air and established annual training for all unites to be conducted at Camp Swift Texas. Since then Adjutant General Sam Turk wanted a more suitable place to assign former Airmen and I wanted an Aviation Battalion. The TXSG Air worked out just fine.

These changes proved to be too much for those who simply wanted to wear the uniform, enjoy the titles and show up once per month. The senior offices closes to me decided to take the side of the few complainers in the field and take whatever steps necessary to block progress, including calling me the "N" word. I looked at the broader picture and felt quite sure that referring to me as one meant minorities in the field of all races were likely to be subject to the same behavior. I informed the Adjutant General Major General Sam Turk and the Office of Governor George W. Bush that it was no longer my pleasure that those very Senior Officers served on my staff.

I recommended Colonel Charles "Rex" Weaver, who currently served on the staff, to replace the first and later recommended Colonel David P. Adloff, Commander of the 19th Regiment, to replace the second. They both became General Officers and served in commendable fashion until my retirement in 1997.

The staff and I would spend the rest of my three-year tenure improving our beloved Guard in any way we could. We revamped the monthly command and staff meeting agenda so instead of the Regimental commanders sitting there listening to the coordinating staff the whole meeting, they were afforded an opportunity to report on their units' activities over the past thirty days. We also began moving every other monthly meeting to Regimental area headquarters throughout the state giving the State Staff an opportunity to see and talk to the Guardsmen whose careers they were entrusted to help manage, the Commanders and Command Sergeants Major gave the new format high ratings.

Replacing the two deputies solved most of my problems, but not all the Adjutants General pitched in by hiring Mr. Williams as Director of the Full-time staff, he was an exceptional administrator and always had my back. One group he could not assist me with was the Association, they continued to take pot shots at me but missed more than they hit. One big hit was when they decided to ignore Ruth and me at the 1994 Annual convention. It was as if they thought I did not know protocol and had not attended any of the previous Conventions where the commander and his spouse were always welcome to sit at the Head table. The following year the State Guard Association of the United States came to town and gave them a lesson in protocol. Not only were we at the head table, because it was held in our state I was the Keynote Speaker.

For fear of sounding too negative in this portion of my memoirs, just let me state that the good outweighed the bad by far and that I would do it all over again.

Of the smart moves I made while Commander, the appointment of Colonel Chet Brooks former Dean of the Senate to Chief of Staff and Sergeants Major Frank G. Deluna, an exceptional airborne soldier to State Command Sergeants Major were among the best. CSM Deluna was the first Hispanic to hold that position. Between the two of them and Colonels Richard Box, John M. Marshall, John L. Newberry, Robert Bodisch and Paul La Velle, I did not have to watch my back as much; we were able to get a staff put together to publish an Annual, featuring the State Headquarters, Seven Regiments, Texas Military Forces Museum and The Association; little did we know that one of the two Governors pictured in the front of that Annual would go on to become President of the United States. I was honored to received packets for possible appointments from the Bush Administration when he was President but my wife did not wish to leave Texas and after thinking it over neither did I. This was still the heaven on earth I imagined it to be, as a child; being told to "wake up – we are in Texas." While listening to the news one day I heard the word Colonias mentioned and remembered hearing my father talk about it when I was a kid. Well these people still did not have water in their community fifty years later. I assigned Colonel John L. Newberry the task of organizing a team, with the responsibility of acquiring the equipment for the building of a well for that community, and letting me know what I could do to help. Colonel Newberry did an exceptional job; although not until after my retirement, was the mission completed at no cost to the government. All equipment needed was donated.

I retired from the State Guard on 8 March 1997 after a total of 32 Federal and State years of my life in uniform.

General Daniel James III, awarded me the Texas Faithful Service Medal upon retirement, because it was the only earnable State award I did not already have. I would spend another ten years teaching at Clear Creek Independent School District, receiving a letter from President and Mrs. George W. Bush upon my retirement in 2007. As I look back in time there are few things I would change, for the lessons I have learned were many and all valuable, and the many students I taught from intermediate to college level and continued to teach at BMI and St. Francis of Assisi Catholic School have enabled me to appreciate even more the teachers and coaches who meant so much to me during my formative years.

CHAPTER TWELVE

People Who Made A Difference

ACROSS THE AGES MANKIND HAS accepted the challenges associated with teaching, guiding and mentoring those in need of leadership. To those whose paths I was fortunate enough to have cross mine. I wholeheartedly give my gratitude, which becomes stronger with time as I realize their importance. I would be remiss if I did not take the time to honor them in a special way. For organizational purposes I have broken them down into five categories. They are My Children, My Village, Peers that made a difference, my Legion of Honor, Band of Angels, and My Texas Military Forces Dream Team.

My Children

Thanks to the two wonderful women whose lives I have been fortunate to share. I have been blessed with eight exceptional young people; whom I consider an honor to have loved, cherished and helped foster their growth and development as they achieved their life goals.

Children

+ Terrance
+ Harriett
+ John III
+ Christopher
+ Yolanda

+ Willie
+ Dee Dee
+ Brian

Grandchildren

- Jarrell
- Quinton
- Ivory
- Cedric

- Malik Jamal
- Brittany
- Taylor

Great Grandchildren

- Jalen Renee (JR)
- Dillon

My Village

The phrase it takes a village said to be from an old African Proverb, pretty much describes my childhood. My father John L. Bailey, my grandmother Betty Johnson Bailey and my Godmother Mrs. Edna Hoxie were the key players of my Village. My mother, whom we lost we I was just two years old, played the most important role by giving me life. The below named people of my Village also reached out and touched me in positive ways. Reverend and Mrs. J. J. Tibbs, Mr. and Mrs. T. A. Looney, Mr. Arthur Phipps, Mr. and Mrs. Buster Crockett, Mr. and Mrs. Sammy Wells Sr., Mr. and Mrs. Robert Atkinson, Sr., Mrs. Willie M. Williams, Mr. and Mrs. Otha Sheridan, Mr. Willie Dean Smith, Mr. and Mrs. George Howell Sr., Mr. and Mrs. James Wattley, Mrs. Opal Watson, Mrs. Bessie Wilhite, Coach and Mrs. Leonard Evans, Coach Mitchell Jackson, Mr. and Mrs. John W. Fenett, Mr. and Mrs. Rueben Johnson, Mr. and Mrs. A. A. Malvern, Mrs. M. Howell Brown, Mrs. Ruth Doty, Mr. and Mrs. Rufus Johnson Sr., Mr. and Mrs. Milton Douglass, Reverend and Mrs. M. L. Bailey, Mrs. Aquilla C. Johnson, Mrs. Wilma Wattley, Reverend Tommy Brown, Mr. and Mrs. Leonard

Wattley, Mrs. And Mrs. Tom Wattley. Mr. and Mrs. Victor L. Threlkeld, Mrs. Peggy White, Mrs. Betty M. Isaac, Mr. and Mrs. Sonny Freeman, Mrs. Irene Blackwell, Mr. and Mrs. James Wattley, Mrs. Christell Reed, Mrs. Wilma Wattley, Mr. and Mrs. Sam Cook, and Ms. Willie Faye Ballard who often talked to me about life after high school and encouraged me to attended college.

Peers

As we age and progress through life so does our peers in early adulthood, we ran five miles together and jumped out of airplanes together, in later years we flew airplanes together as student pilots and as Army Aviators in Vietnam and finally we became Educators and business owners. I'm grateful to them all for our dialogue and their friendship. They were Raymond Freeman, Ralph Shaw, Johnny Wilson, Monk Montgomery, Freddie L. Johnson, Troy G. Baker, David Adloff, Robert Brandenberg, Gerry Thames, Craig King, Bob Butterworth, Melvin Starks, Robert Myers, Gary Sellman, J. P. Best III, Ruppert Sargent, J. W. Hendrix, Dean Anderson, Bob Lapan, Herbert Keaty, Duke Bodisch, John Carrigan, Corky Smith, Leon Butler, Roy Riddle, Larry Reams, Major Smith of Unified Veterans of America, Bernard Gunn, Art Nichols, Tom Everhart, William Magee, Lloyd Hill, Lemarse Washington, Luther Berry, Bernard Belvin, Lenny Leassear, Andrea Morrison, Carry Ross, Lillie Williams, Malcolm Wharton, Tom Erby, Ben Troutman, General Neasman, whose first name really is "General," Dr. Charles Glass, Ned Salter, Johnny Wilson, Fred Lewis, Daniel James III, Sam Turk, Marlin Mote, Cliff Robinson, Chet Brooks, Karl McLeod, Anthony Hall, Jim Robinson, Joe Bailey, John Echoff, Craig Roberts, Bill Daws, Wild Bill James, Charlie

Woodson, Joe Rossignol, Vernon Baker, Tasjah Hall and Sharon Hudson, Bruce Harris, Daryl Smith, Willie Bratcher, Bernard Banks, Ralph Johnson and Ken Kubasik.

Many of my peers who made a difference in my life were successful to an extent of epic proportions. My failure to mention their titles in this section means they are all of equal importance in my life; thank you for your example, your candor and your willingness to stand by me at those points in my life when the road turned or threatened to turn, and for just allowing me to be a part of your lives.

My Legion Of Honor;
Friends Lost In Combat

John 5:13 reads "Greater love has no one than this, that he lay down his life for his friends. It only takes a small stretch of the imagination for the word friends to parallel the word compatriots." Therefore I choose this verses as a lead into honor a very special group, that I call my "Legion of Honor." Their courage will remain unquestioned and their sacrifice matched by few;

+ Lieutenant Ruppert Sargent, Vietnam, Medal of Honor Recipient
+ Lieutenant Freddie L. Johnson, Vietnam Soldiers Medal Recipient
+ Lieutenant Gary A. Scott; 101st Airborne Division Vietnam 1968
+ Lieutenant Michael L. Gandy; 101st Airborne Division Vietnam 1968
+ Lieutenant Frank L. Rodriguez; 101st Airborne Division Vietnam 1968
+ Lieutenant Frank Stallings; Vietnam
+ Captain Lee P. Grimsley, "Green Eyes I" Vietnam

+ Sergeant Florian Zahn, Vietnam Silver Star, 101st Airborne Division, 1968
+ Private First Class Danny Braswell, Vietnam
+ Private First Class Russell Milberry, Vietnam, 101st Airborne Division, 1968
+ Specialist 4 Michael Herrera, Vietnam, 101st Airborne Division, 1968
+ Captain Caldwell
+ First Sergeant Lutz, 101st Airborne Division, 1968
+ 1st Lieutenant Johnson in a Chinook crash, from the 1st Aviation Brigade, 1972
+ Lieutenant Price; Officer Candidate – friend, Aberdeen Proving Ground, MD
+ Lieutenant Stark Officer Candidate – friend, Aberdeen Proving Grounds, MD

GUARDIAN ANGELS

I believe that those who have gone on before us create a web of protection around us seeking only our safety, success and peace of mind; to list all my protectors would be another stand alone book, therefore, I will simply list some of the most recent to join my Band of Angels:

+ Lucille Clark Bailey
+ John L. Bailey
+ Reverend John H. Bailey
+ Velma Johnson Bailey
+ Mabelle Bailey Freeman
+ Betty Johnson Bailey
+ Edna Wattley Hoxie

- Reverend J. J. Tibbs
- Ethel Wells
- Izora Wattley Tibbs
- Yolanda Ellis (our Daughter)
- Terrance Ellis (our Son)
- Coach Mitchell Jackson
- Rufus Johnson, Sr.
- Aquilla Johnson
- Robert Atkinson, Sr.
- Freddie L. Johnson
- Florian Zahn
- Ruppert Sargent
- Lee Grimsley
- Gary A. Scott
- Danny Brasswell
- Michael L. Gandy
- Gloria J. Betts
- Charles Jackson Harris
- Susie Stingley
- Harold Laranang

MY DREAM TEAM

My accomplishments while Commander of the State Guard would not have been possible without the loyalty, devotion and tireless efforts of many members of the headquarters Staff who wanted the Unit to do what good and decent people expect organizations to do regardless to the race, creed, or color of the person chosen to lead. They want to see improvement, professionalism, and fairness; My Dream Team at Camp Mabry:

+ Brigadier General David P. Adloff, Deputy Commander
+ Brigadier Charles R. Weaver; Deputy Commander
+ Colonel Karl B. McLeod, Chief of Staff
+ Colonel Chet Brooks; Chief of Staff and G2
+ Colonel Richard Box
+ CSM Heinrich Sailer
+ CSM Frank Deluna
+ Colonel Robert J. Bodisch, Sr.
+ Colonel Thomas W. Anderson G3 Operations and Training
+ Colonel John P. Echoff; G4 Logistics
+ Colonel John L. Newberry; G5 Public Affairs
+ Lieutenant Colonel Thomas W. Johnson; Chaplain
+ Colonel John Carrigan
+ Ms. Claudette Neumann, Secretary
+ Colonel John M. Marshall; Inspector General
+ Colonel John W. Schiesser; Staff Judge Advocate
+ Colonel Bernard Belvin

+ Colonel Nolan Stone
+ Colonel Bob Miller
+ CW2 Lloyd Sanchez
+ Mr. Ricky Williams
+ CSM Paul Esler
+ Lieutenant Colonel Paul La Valle
+ Major Wayne Bounds; Historian
+ Major Wayne Stokes; Staff Member
+ Major Valentine Belfiglio; Historian

Aide de Camps:
+ Lieutenant Willie B. Williams
+ Lieutenant Kevin Reams
+ Lieutenant Steven Crowe
+ Mr. Williams, Director TXSG
+ Captain Johnnie Jones, Aide de Camp to Major General Marlin Mote

FOUR LEGGED FAMILY
+ Brown Eye
+ Snoopy
+ Othello (Killer)
+ Desdemona (Little Bit)
+ Queen (Killer's Daughter)
+ Poochie
+ Yolanda (Yogi)
+ Cheyenne

CHALLENGE

To fly an airplane is my goal
I'm not smart enough I've been told
Brains and guts are what I lack
Mainly because my face is black.

I asked my father if this was true
He said I wouldn't worry if I were you
Just set your goals and set them high
And let them lift you to the sky.

Next time my father went to town
A book about airmen, somehow he found
It told of men some black some fair
Who met their glory in the air.

I read through tears
As chills raced my back....
My God I smiled....
These pilots are black

Library of Congress Registration number 3-567-090 Written in 1949 by
John H. Bailey, II as an eight year old.

The Bailey Family Crest was drawn by my father John L. Bailey in 1954.

More About the Author

AWARDS AND DECORATIONS

Soldiers Medal (for Heroism in the Republic of Viet Nam)

Bronze Star (with Oak Leaf Cluster)

Meritorious Service Medal

Air Medal (with Oak Leaf Clusters)

Army Commendation Medal (with 2 "V" Devices for Heroism and 2 Oak Leaf Clusters)

National Defense Service Medal

Armed Forces Reserve Medal (with Silver Hour Glass)

Good Conduct Medal (Third Award)

Vietnam Campaign Medal (with Seven Campaign Stars)

Army Service Ribbon

Vietnam Cross of Gallantry (with Palm, Individual Award)

Vietnam Service Ribbon

Lone Star Distinguished Service Medal

Texas Outstanding Service Medal

Texas Medal of Merit

Adjutant General's Individual Award (with 2 Stars)

Texas Faithful Service Medal

Texas State Guard Service Medal

Army Aviators Badge

Senior Parachutist Badge

Expert Rifleman Badge

State Guard Staff Identification Badge

EFFECTIVE DATES OF PROMOTION

Second Lieutenant 10 May 1967

First Lieutenant 10 May 1968

Captain 10 May 1969

Major 31 March 1979

Lieutenant Colonel 23 September 1986

Colonel 14 May 1988

Brigadier General 25 January 1991

Major General 12 February 1994

EDUCATION

Embry Riddle Aeronautical University, B.S.

Alcorn State University, M.Ed.

Command And Generals Staff College

Organizations

Masonic Lodge
Sigma Chi, "Significant Sig"
Fort Bend County Sigma Chi Alumni Chapter
Brothers of the Wind, Founding Member
Men for Change
Unified Veterans of America, Chairman of the Board
Veteran of Foreign Wars
Bronze Eagles Flying Club
Triple Nickel (555) Airborne Association, Life Member
USAA
Black Pilots of America
National Guards Association of Texas, Life Member
Military Officers Association of America, Life Member
State Guard Association of the United States

Printed in the United States
By Bookmasters